THE TRUE MASONIC EXPERIENCE

A closer look on how to improve the Masonic Experience of your members.

1st Edition - 2017

Roberto M. Sanchez, 32° K∴C∴C∴H∴, K.Y.C.H

Past Master, Gray Lodge No. 329 A.F. & A.M. - Texas

Past Master, St Albans Lodge No. 1455 A.F. & A.M. - Texas

The True Masonic Experience
First Edition, Published 2017
Copyright © 2017 Roberto M. Sanchez

ISBN 978-0-9990596-3-0

Printed in the USA by
RMS Publishing
Sugar Land, TX

Cover: Picture of the Gray Lodge No. 329 altar by Bill Bradford

Portrait of Roberto M. Sanchez by Travis Simpkins

Dedication

To my dear friends and brothers who have shown me the vision of what it is to be a True Mason and be part of a True Masonic Experience. Those whom I consider to be my mentors and teachers in Masonry and in Life, I have been very fortunate to call you, not just a mentor, but also a friend. In grateful appreciation and acknowledgement of many years of trust and friendship, this book is dedicated to you.

Pierre G. " Pete" Normand 33°, Past Grand Chancellor of the Grand College of Rites, who is the charter Worshipful Master and master mind behind St Alban's Lodge No. 1455 and what is known today as the Traditional Observant Movement.

Rex R. Hutchens 33° GC, author of a Bridge to Light and Pillars of Wisdom. Past Grand Master of the Grand Lodge of Arizona. Past Grand High Priest of the Grand Chapter R.A.M. of Arizona, Past Grand Master of the Grand Council of R. & S. M. of Arizona. Past Grand Commander of Arizona.

About the Author

Roberto M. Sanchez is a very active Freemason. He served as Worshipful Master of his Mother Lodge - Gray Lodge No. 329 in 2011-2012, and as District Deputy Grand Master in 2013. In 2013-2014, he served as President of the Master's Warden's and Secretaries Association of the 30th District in Houston, Texas. That same year he served as Worshipful Master of St Albans' Lodge No 1455, a Traditional Observance Lodge in College Station, Texas. He also served as Secretary of Gray Lodge No 329 for many years.

Roberto is a member of the Houston Scottish Rite where he is a 32° (K.C.C.H.) Knight Commander of the Court of Honor; and served as Commander for the Council of Kadosh in 2014. In 2009, 2011and 2013 he was aid to the Sovereign Grand Commander, Ronald A. Seal, during the Supreme Council session. Roberto is also a member of the York Rite, where he has served as presiding officer of Washington Chapter No. 2, Houston Council No. 1 and Ruthven Commandery No. 2. As a result of presiding with distinction he was invited into the Knight York Cross of Honor (K.Y.C.H.) Roberto is also a member of Chinar Grotto M.O.V.P.E.R. where he served as Monarch, the presiding officer in 2013.

For his dedication to the Craft, Roberto has been invited to several honorary and invitational bodies such as: The Societas Rosicruciana in Civitatibus Foederatis (SRICF), where he is currently the Celebrant for Stella Sola College in Texas. Gulf Coast York Rite College No. 106 where he is currently serving in the advancing line. Lone Star Chapel No. 5 Commemorative Order of St. Thomas of Acon where he is currently serving in the advancing line. Sam Houston Council Allied Masonic Degrees No. 275

where he served as Sovereign Master in 2013 and Anson Jones Council of Knight Masons No. 47 where he served as Excellent Chief in 2016. In 2017, he was awarded the Knight Commander of Zerubbabel by the Grand Council of Knight Masons USA. He also belongs to the Royal Order of Scotland, the Grand College of Rites and several other bodies.

Roberto has given lectures on Masonry all over the United States and across Latin America, Canada and Europe. Because of his love for history and Masonic research, Roberto joined several research lodges including Texas Lodge of Research, where he has presented various papers and therefore elected as a full member and served as Junior Warden. Roberto was the original Curator, Historian and Librarian for the Houston Masonic Library Museum and served on the Board of Directors and Executive Committee.

Roberto M. Sanchez   Travis Simpkins 2017

AUDI, VIDE, TACE.

"WHAT WE HAVE DONE FOR OURSELVES ALONE DIES
WITH US; WHAT WE HAVE DONE FOR OTHERS AND
THE WORLD REMAINS AND IS IMMORTAL".

– ALBERT PIKE 33°, SOVEREIGN GRAND
COMMANDER A.A.S.R. SJ 1859-1891

Table of Contents

Foreword

Masons can consider this a title that delivers on its promise.

Roberto Sanchez takes the reader on a journey often bypassed in mainstream American Freemasonry. His extensive involvement and participation in the fraternity, supplemented by his wide-ranging travels through the United States, Canada, Europe and Latin America, positions him as not only a well-traveled Mason, but one who constructively absorbed his experiences. Those experiences bolster his qualifications to speak with expertise and understanding of Freemasonry as an "Initiative Art" and address areas missing from our Craft for decades.

As he notes, for generations many Masons have convinced themselves that today's common practices represent what has been practiced since time immemorial. Unfortunately, they are often not. Veering away from our foundations in this way has inevitably weakened the aim, purpose and heritage of the Craft. Freemasonry in the United States is increasingly vulnerable because of that drift.

The author provides crucial information for Masons seeking more than what may have merely been handed down to them by their respective lodge cultures. The breadth and depth of our rich heritage and how the entire system of Freemasonry serves as a blueprint to be practiced in its entirety - not just its convenient parts - is a point well-made and made often.

The collection of topics covered by Brother Sanchez offers a treasure trove of details. His explanations of heritage practices and contextual background on their origins is punctuated by his plain talk. The positive results of restoring such practices in his own lodge - where there was a collective determination to return to heritage-driven features - stands as a poignant example of the slow and much needed return to the original promise of Freemasonry to its votaries.

This work is a welcome contribution to the literature required by every generation of men involved in Freemasonry, but particularly those men today who seek more than the ordinary and the heritage-driven Masonic experience.

John Bizzack, Ph.D.
Lexington Lodge No. 1, Lexington, KY
The Rubicon Masonic Society

Preface

While this book is for the use of Masons and Masonic Lodges for the purposes of educating and enhancing the experience of their members, there is nothing secret within this book that could not be shared with a non-Mason. Masonry is a peculiar institution, and everything discussed within the confines of this book has been practiced in Masonic Lodges all over the world at some point. The purpose of this book is to allow Freemason, new and old an opportunity to learn and experience some of the practices that have fallen out of custom in our lodges.

This book starts by giving you a brief historical explanation of several important events in the United States – all of which involved prominent Freemasons. This is personally one of the reasons that I was attracted to the Craft. I was impressed by how many honorable men of great importance were Freemasons. My thinking was that these men were great because they were Freemasons, or they were attracted to the organization because of the greatness it gave its members. Either way it was something that I wanted to be part of and be considered among its members. It is truly amazing how many aspects of this country's history is immersed with Freemasonry, and not just here but all over the world.

However, once I joined I could not help to feel like I was missing something. I could not believe some of the greatest men in history would have attended lodge and had the lackluster experience I originally had. There was something not quite right, and I was correct. I was missing out on the actual experience I expected from such an honorable institution. I therefore went in search of that experience, in my quest of attaining more light. Shortly thereafter, I was pleasantly surprised to find such an experience existed within the fraternity. However, I was disappointed in some of the leaders of the fraternity, in their lack to help making this experience available to its members. Most were more concerned with declining membership or worrying about non-members. In business, if your customers are not pleased with their experience with you, why on earth would they come back. Before you worry about getting new customers, you need to be concerned in making the ones you already have happy.

The lack of empathy and understanding as to what such a great problem this is disturbs me to this day. Nevertheless, I made it my quest to bring this experience to the members of my lodge. When I became a Master Mason, the average attendance at my mother lodge was about 15 to 20, with a membership of 350. The next year I became an officer of the lodge, and we began to implement some of these practices. By the time I was Master of the lodge a few years later, the lodge had completely transformed. The average attendance was in the 80's, with one meeting having 132 in attendance. Those Masons were not there to see me; they were there because of the experience the lodge was offering.

That is were this book continues, introducing you to the practices, principles, and traditions that will allow your members to have a True Masonic Experience. I cannot guarantee the same results as my lodge, but I can tell you the experience you will have at your lodge will change for the better.

It is my greatest hope that Masons reconsider bringing all of these obscure traditions back to mainstream Masonry and re-dignify the institution of Freemasonry to the great institution it was intended to be. While it is imperative for all Masons to follow and abide by the rules and regulations under who's jurisdiction they may be, discussing and changing these regulations is always a possibility. Talk to your Grand Lodge or the representatives from your lodge and ask for clarification in all of these matters. If your jurisdiction forbids or discourage its members from doing any of these, by all means remain true to your obligation. However, I do encourage you to propose a resolution to rectify or remedy this. Masonry is here to make good men better, and while this is done though our allegories and lessons, it is up to us to translate that on to our members. We owe it to them to give them Masonry, which is what they are asking for. Since you are going to give them that why not make it the best experience possible, why not give them *The True Masonic Experience.*

Introduction

This book is brought to you in the spirit of Traditional Masonry, Traditional being that of the beginning origins of Speculative Freemasonry. Unfortunately, Traditional Freemasonry is not the norm in American Masonic Lodges today. Several of our most honorable and ancient traditions are not being practiced in most of our lodges; even in several cases they are illegal in some Masonic jurisdictions. In so many lodges today, the real intent of a True Masonic Experience is not being observed. We have diverted away from what our forefathers originally intended, and have become satisfied with the mediocre fellowship endured over a spaghetti dinner on paper plates, pancake breakfasts and fish fry's. This is not Freemasonry! Why is it that we as Freemasons have tried to turn masonry into something that it is not, and have veered away from some of the foundations of the order? Why is it ok for us to create innovations in Freemasonry despite the fact that it is forbidden in the ancient charges? Moreover, we have convinced ourselves that what we have turned the craft into, is what has been practiced since time immemorial. I – by no means consider myself the premiere authority on the subject. However, I have traveled to over 70 different masonic jurisdictions – and I have experienced the True Masonic Experience. It is my hope to share that experience with you, with the hope that this book will aid you to achieve the True Masonic Experience for you and the members of your Lodge.

Chapter One
THE SQUARE THE COMPASSES AND THE UNITED STATES

The Square and Compasses is one of the most recognized symbols in the world, and just as the Cross has a significance and represents Christianity, the Square and Compasses represent Freemasonry. The Square and Compasses or Freemasonry, the fraternal order they represent are extensively seen throughout the 230-plus year history of the United States. All through the vast and enlightening history of the United States, there have been numerous amounts of legendary episodes involving the Freemasons. There are Masonic symbols everywhere in the United States, from the unfinished pyramid and the All-

Seeing Eye on the back of the one-dollar Federal Reserve

Note to the Great Seal of the United States, and even in the

Texas and United States flags. In 1844, George K. Teulon,

Grand Secretary of Grand Lodge of the Republic of Texas,

addressed a gathering of Masons in Portland, Maine and

explained why Texas picked the Lone Star as the National

Emblem.

> Texas is empathically a Masonic Country: Our
> National Emblem, The Lone Star, was chosen from
> among the emblems selected by Freemasonry to
> illustrate the five moral virtues – it is a five pointed
> star, and alludes to the five points of fellowship[1].

From our laws to our buildings and even in our

Constitution, the presence of the Square and Compasses

has been present. Two of the greatest documents ever

written in American history were constructed and based on

the teachings of Freemasonry. The United States

Constitution was written in part and signed by at least

thirteen Freemasons; as well as the Declaration of

Independence, which at least nine known Freemasons

signed, including John Hancock and Benjamin Franklin. Of course, one cannot forget about the several Masonic buildings and monuments and their dedications. For instance, the Washington Monument and the George Washington Masonic National Memorial are both Masonic structures. A Masonic cornerstone laying was held for the Statue of Liberty, sculpted by Frederic Auguste Bartholi, a Master Mason from France, on 5 August 1884. Mount Rushmore was sculpted by father and son Gutzon and Lincoln Borglum, both Master Masons. Lincoln Borglum was raised in Battle River Lodge No. 92 at Hermosa, South Dakota, and Gutzon Borglum in Howard Lodge No. 35 in New York City. The San Jacinto monument as well as the world-renowned United States Capitol building also had a Masonic cornerstone dedication ceremony on 18 September 1793, led by George Washington, a Master Mason[2].

Freemasonry is a fraternity or society whose membership is restricted exclusively to men. The Masonic

Order is a serious group that bases its principles and teachings on the goal of taking a good man and helping him become a better man. However, Freemasonry is not an improvement society, nor was it created to reform criminals or people of low standards. Such a person would not benefit from Masonic teachings, nor even be taken into consideration for membership. The ritual and initiation of candidates conducted within each lodge is still the same that has been practiced for hundreds of years. Every Mason on earth has been led through the same traditions and instructed in the same mysteries and secrets. Freemasonry is considered by many to be a secret society but that is not the case: Freemasonry is not a secret organization. If it were, the buildings would not be easily identified and its members would not wear rings and other jewelry with the familiar Square and Compasses emblem. Freemasonry is a society with secrets, like secret handshakes and other ways to distinguish themselves from non-Masons, and conducts meetings only open to members of the order, just as many other fraternities or orders do.

Although the actual origins of Freemasonry are clouded in the mists of antiquity, it is widely agreed that Masonry dates back to the late fourteenth century and flourished during the middle ages when guilds of Masons traveled throughout Europe, building the great Gothic Cathedrals. Masonry developed from lodges of operative or stonemasons[3].

The Masonry of today is distinguished from the old stonemasonry by being referred to as "Speculative" Masonry. Speculative, or Freemasonry, does not work with stone but rather works on the lives of men. Its teachings take the imagery of carpentry, architecture, and stonemasonry and use those images with the assistance of symbols to instruct and promote the building of a good moral character. The Mason from the Grand Lodge of Texas uses this imagery:

The trowel is an instrument made use of by operative Masons to spread the cement which unites a building in one common mass; but we, as Free and Accepted Masons, are taught to make use of it for the more noble and glorious purpose of spreading the cement of brotherly love and affection; that cement which unites us into one sacred band, or society of friends and brothers, among whom no contention should ever exist, but that noble contention, or rather emulation, of who can best work and best agree.[4]

In working or operative stonemasonry, apprentices were taken in and taught the craft by master masons who passed on the secrets of the trade. As this trade declined, the guilds began to accept members who were not actually stonemasons. From these roots evolved Masonry as we know it today.

The oldest Masonic document, the Regius poem, dates to around 1390 A.D. There is no documentation of Freemasonry before that, but Freemasonry is believed by some to be dated back to the building of King Solomon's Temple. Somewhere between 1390 and 1717, lodges of operative masons began to accept other men who did not work in the building trade as members. Eventually entire lodges composed of such people sprang up, leading to a transition from lodges being composed of stonemasons to lodges of men from other occupations who gathered and shared a ritual replete with allusions to carpentry, architecture, and stonemasonry. In 1717, four of these lodges in England assembled at the Goose and Gridiron Alehouse and formed the first Grand Lodge-The Most Worshipful Grand Lodge of England. A Grand Lodge is a Masonic body having jurisdiction over the lodges within a certain geographical area. Every state in the U.S., including the District of Columbia, and almost every country in the world, has a Grand Lodge, which in some way derived from the first Grand Lodge, The United Grand Lodge of England [5].

Freemasonry was brought to America by the colonists in the 18th century and was well established throughout the continents of North and South America by 1820. The advent of lodges charted by The Grand Lodge of England and other European Grand Lodges began prior to 1730, but the first Grand Lodge in the New World was The Grand Lodge of Massachusetts dating back to 1733. The first Grand Lodge in the Americas was formally organized under the leadership of Henry Price and met at the Bunch of Grapes Tavern in Boston, Massachusetts. The Masonic craze quickly spread throughout the colonies and the search for Masonic Light was greatly sought after. "It is undeniable that many of the philosophies written into the Declaration of Independence and the United States Constitution were talked about and practiced long before, in Masonic lodges" The quest for Masonic knowledge, and the curiosity of what stood behind the Square and Compasses, enlisted many men into the fraternity and influenced their lives.[6]

During the Revolutionary War, influence of the Square and Compasses was ubiquitous. Many of America's early patriots were Masons, including George Washington, Benjamin Franklin, John Hancock, James Otis, James Monroe, Robert Livingston and Samuel Adams, among many others. America's most famous Mason, George Washington, who said the Order's goal was to "promote the happiness of the human race,"[7] favored the creation of military Lodges for soldiers. There were eleven such Lodges, the most famous one being American Union Lodge Number One. George Washington was made a Mason at the age of twenty in Fredericksburg Lodge, in Fredericksburg Virginia on 4 November 1752. He was raised to the sublime degree of a Master Mason on 4 August 1753, and eventually became Master of his lodge and even proposed as Grand Master of a Military United Grand Lodge in Morristown[8]. Washington took his oath of office for The United States Presidency on a Masonic Bible, personally delivered by Robert Livingston, Grand Master of the Grand Lodge of New York.

Next to George Washington, the most celebrated person to wear the Square and Compasses proudly was Benjamin Franklin. Benjamin Franklin was one of the most recognized figures in American history: he was a signer of the Declaration of Independence and of the United States Constitution, as well as one of the creators of the Great Seal of the United States. Franklin was a diplomat, publisher and inventor and would become one of America's most prominent Freemasons. Franklin was initiated in February of 1730 at St. John's Lodge, which met at Tun Tavern, and by 1734 Franklin was Worshipful Master of his lodge. Franklin became Grand Master in 1749 and 1760 for both Pennsylvania and Massachusetts. Because of his affiliation with an A.F. & A. M. Grand Lodge and an F. & A. M. Grand

Lodge, Franklin was denied a Masonic Funeral by both

Grand Lodges. At the time the Ancient Freemasons (A.

F. & A. M.) and the Modern Freemasons (F. & A. M.)

were in dispute over who was traditionally correct and

properly sanctioned.[9]

The Square and Compasses, along with the purple

of the fraternity, were suspended from the breast and rested

on the honored shoulders of some of America's greatest

early patriots. Joseph Warren, Paul Revere, and Samuel

Adams were all Grand Masters of the Grand Lodge of

Massachusetts, and Robert Livingston was Grand Master of

the Grand Lodge of New York. General Joseph Warren,

who gave his life at the Battle of Bunker Hill in June of

1775, was the Grand Master of The Most Worshipful

Grand Lodge of Massachusetts at the time of his death. The

British threw his partially decapitated remains into a

shallow unmarked grave; his body was later identified

because of a molar that Paul Revere made for Warren. The

molar was quite peculiar, being that Revere carved a square and compass on it; therefore, it was easily recognizable. Upon recovering Warren's lifeless remains, members of St. Andrews Lodge gave Grand Master Warren a proper Masonic Burial.[10]

Paul Revere was one of the first York Rite Freemasons in the U.S. when he became a Royal Arch Mason and Knight Templar on 11 December 1769. Revere's most notable contribution in the Revolutionary War was his famous midnight ride from Lexington to Concord on 18 April 1775. Revere received a signal from the bell tower of North Church, "one if by land, two if by sea," to warn the colonists that the British were coming. Revere also served as Most Worshipful Grand Master of The Grand Lodge of Massachusetts, A. F. & A. M. from 1794 – 1797.[11]

Robert Livingston may not be as well remembered in the history books as some of his fellow Masons, but in his day, he was more celebrated than Paul Revere was. Livingston was on the original committee that drafted the Declaration of Independence. Livingston was also a United States minister to France and helped negotiate the Louisiana Purchase. In addition to this, Livingston was also a close personal friend of Napoleon. Robert Livingston's most famous Masonic episode was when he administrated George Washington's oath of office for the presidency of the United States, using the Masonic altar bible from St. Johns lodge No. 1. At that time Livingston was the Most Worshipful Grand Master of The Grand Lodge of New York, F. & A.M. as well as a Past Master and member of Union Lodge in New York City.[12]

Freemasonry, with its emphasis on brotherhood, enlisted many leading colonial Americans who saw Freemasonry as a vehicle for establishing the principles of liberty and equality. Its teachings helped spread a tremendous patriotic movement. For example, Some historians believe that the "Indians" who took part in the Boston Tea Party were Masons from Boston's St. Andrews Lodge. Samuel Adams was a member of St. Andrews Lodge, which at the time met at The Green Dragon Tavern in Boston, Massachusetts. Adams also served as Most Worshipful Grand Master of The Grand Lodge of Massachusetts, A. F. & A. M. It is believed that on 16 December 1773, on the day of a lodge meeting, a group of Masons were observed following Sam Adams to the Green Dragon Tavern, the meeting place of St. Andrews Lodge. Several minutes later about fifty "Indians" were seen leaving from the tavern and heading for Griffin's wharf. Once the wharf was reached the "Indians" climbed aboard the ships *Eleanor, Darthmouth*, and the *Beaver* and cracked opened 342 tea chests weighing about 45 tons and dumped them overboard into the harbor.[13] By dawn an estimated worth of 10, 000 British pounds had been cast into the waters of Boston harbor. Out of all of the "Indians" who participated in the Boston Tea Party, more than seventy-five percent have been proven to be Masons.[14] Freemasons have access to private tiled meetings which only allow Master Masons if they are properly clothed and vouched for. The secretary is only permitted to make a correct record of things proper to be written. With these incentives, it becomes easy to plan a historical event such as this, and to an extent, it becomes difficult to prove whether many of those historic events were planned at a Masonic meeting. Perhaps this is Masonic secrecy in action.

In 1803, President Thomas Jefferson and French Dictator Napoleon Bonaparte signed a treaty known most commonly as The Louisiana Purchase. This treaty allowed the United States to purchase the Louisiana Territory, containing 504 million acres, from the French for 15 million dollars, roughly three cents an acre. The origins of Thomas Jefferson's affiliation to the craft have been disputed by several historians due to the lack of evidence.

Although there is no actual record of his affiliation to a

Masonic Lodge, there is record of him being in attendance

at Masonic events, such as the cornerstone laying at the

University of Virginia. Napoleon, however, was made a

Mason on 12 June 1795 in Army Philadelphe Lodge, in

Malta.[14]. Napoleon's brother Joseph Bonaparte became

Grand Master for the Grand Lodge of France in 1805. The

purchase of the Louisiana Territory was the beginning of

Masonry's expansion to the west: By June of 1803,

President Jefferson sent two explorers, Meriwether Lewis

and William Clark on an expedition to the Louisiana

Territory. Lewis and Clark were both Masons and

members of the same lodge, St. Louis Lodge No 111. By

1817 the idea of Manifest Destiny, America reaching the

Pacific Ocean, "from sea to shining sea," started by Mason

and President James Monroe, was well underway. Lewis

and Clark's exploration allowed many Americans to move

to the newly mapped-out west, which developed into the

creation of territories such as Texas. "In 1821, young

Stephen F. Austin negotiated with the territorial governor

in San Antonio to start a colony in Texas populated by

slave-owning, white Americans."[15]

Stephen F. Austin came to Texas to fulfill his

father's undertakings and to find a life of prosperity. In

1815, Austin was made a Mason in Louisiana Lodge No.

109 in Genevieve, Missouri, the first lodge west of the

Mississippi[16]. Austin later transferred his membership to St.

Louis Lodge No. 111, where Meriwether Lewis and

William Clark where members. In 1822, while meeting

with officials in Mexico City, Stephen F. Austin became

friends with Lorenzo de Zavala along with other influential

and important Mexican Masons in the Mexican

Government. Lorenzo De Zavala would later become one

of the men who signed the Texas Declaration of

Independence. De Zavala also took an active part in

establishing York Rite Masonry in Mexico and became the

Charter Master of Independencia Lodge No. 454. On 11

February 1828, Austin, along with H. H. League, Thomas

M. Duke, Eli Mitchell, Ira Ingram, Joseph White, and G. B.

Hall arranged a meeting at San Felipe in order to petition

the York Grand Lodge of Mexico for the charter of a Texas

Lodge. The petition eventually reached Mexico and the

York Grand Lodge of Mexico refused the charter.

Freemasonry's legendary U.S. crisis came in 1826

when an ex–Mason, William Morgan, disappeared after

publishing his exposé of Masonry. The disappearance of

Captain William Morgan raised the awareness of the

activities of Freemasons in the United States in the 1820s.

This caused some changes in Freemasonry as well as in the

United States politics, in the election of 1828 and 1832.

Masons were accused of kidnapping Morgan, and in the

resulting furor, the Anti-Masonic Party was formed. In

1832, the Anti-Masonic party ran a presidential candidate,

William Wirt, against Andrew Jackson, Past Grand Master

of the Grand Lodge of Tennessee and a member of St. Tammany No. 29 in Nashville. Wirt carried only the state of Vermont and nothing else and soon the Anti-Masonic party died out. Andrew Jackson became the seventh President of the United States: Jackson received his Masonic degrees in Harmony Lodge No. 1 in Tennessee and was Grand Master of The Most Worshipful Grand Lodge of Tennessee from 1822 –1824[17]. After 1832, Freemasonry began to lose its political position, taking on the social and more emphatically fraternal character it has today. This helped its steady growth; there were 200,000 members [of the order] when the Civil War began in 1861. During the war, over a hundred military lodges were formed. After the Civil War, these lodges helped in the Order's period of great growth. By 1900, there were over 800,000 members worldwide, and by the year 2000, there were over 5 million estimated members worldwide.

The birth of Masonry in Texas actually came on 10 March 1835, when six Masons decided to meet under what is now known as the Masonic Oak in Brazoria. Anson Jones, John Wharton, Asa Brigham, Alexander Russell, J.P. Caldwell and James Phelps met in seclusion under the Masonic Oak and decided to petition the Grand Lodge of Louisiana for the dispensation of a new Lodge[18]. The most prominent Mason at this gathering was Anson Jones; later in his life, he would become the last President of the Republic of Texas, the first Worshipful Master of Holland Lodge No. 1, and the first Most Worshipful Grand Master of the Grand Lodge of Texas A.F. & A.M. The dispensation was granted and the first Lodge in Texas was born and named Holland Lodge No. 36, in Honor of John Henry Holland, Grand Master of the Grand Lodge of Louisiana, which chartered the first three lodges in Texas. The first meeting of Holland Lodge No. 36 was conducted on 27 December 1835. Holland Lodge No. 36 later became known as Holland Lodge No. 1 once the Grand Lodge of Texas was established on 20 December 1837 in Houston, Texas. Holland Lodge struggled during the Texas Revolution; especially when the Mexican army, led by General Jose de Urea, destroyed most of the lodges records and equipment. Because of these reasons, the members of Holland Lodge decided not to settle in Brazoria, but moved to Houston in October of 1837. Holland Lodge No. 1 is now located on 4911 Montrose Boulevard in Houston, Texas.

The Grand Lodge of Louisiana issued two additional charters to Texas Lodges in 1837-1838: Milam No. 40 at Nacogdoches and McFarland No. 41 in San Augustine. In December 1837, delegates from these three lodges convened in Houston to organize the Grand Lodge of the Republic of Texas. President Sam Houston presided over this meeting, which resulted in the election of Anson Jones as the first Grand Master[19].

Between 1838 and 1845, the Texas Grand Lodge issued charters to twenty-one more lodges, and membership increased from seventy-three to 357. In addition, there were probably some 1,100 Masons from other jurisdictions living in Texas at this time. Although constituting only one and a half percent of the total population, Masons filled some eighty percent of the Republic's higher offices. All of the presidents, vice presidents, and secretaries of state of the Republic of Texas were Masons. After annexation, Masons continued to be equally prominent in the state government; between 1846 and 1861, five of the six governors were members of the fraternity.

During President Andrew Jackson's administration, in 1835, Mexico imposed stricter controls of Texas. When the Mexican Government became totally unbearable Texas declared its independence and the war between Texas and Mexico began. There were many Masons in chief positions of authority, both political and military in the war for Texas independence. The war finally broke out when the Mexican Military led by Fransico de Castañeda arrived in Texas in the fall of 1835; they demanded the Anglos return a cannon given to them by the Mexican Government to help protect themselves from Indian attacks. The first shot of the war was fired by Eli Mitchell on 2 October 1835 near Gonzalez, by the very same cannon the Mexican army was there to retrieve. Mitchell and his commander, Colonel John Moore, were both Masons. Eli Mitchell was made a Mason in Somerset Lodge No. 84 in Somerset County Pennsylvania in 1821. He was initiated in October, passed in November and raised a Master Mason in December.[20]

The Mission of San Antonio de Valero, better known as the Alamo, was the birthplace of Freemasonry in west Texas. William B. Travis, James Bowie, David Crockett, and other Masons who were stationed at the Alamo, held Masonic meetings in the Alamo[21]. William B. Travis was raised to the sublime degree of a Master Mason in Alabama Lodge No. 3; James Bowie received his Masonic degrees in Humble Cottage Lodge No. 19, and proof that David Crockett was a Mason is based mainly on the survival of a Masonic Apron that is said to have belonged to him[22]. On 6 March 1836, after a thirteen-day siege, the Alamo fell to the Mexican army led by Mexican dictator, "the Napoleon of the West," General Antonio Lopez de Santa Anna, a one-time member of The Grand Lodge of the Valley of Mexico. Among the 188 Texan and Tejano soldiers that died on that day, a few were known Masons and some others were thought to be Masons. Alamo Lodge holds a stated meeting every year inside the Alamo to commemorate those Brethren who died there. Two plaques were also placed on the south wall of the barracks in the Alamo for the same reason.

Sam Houston became Commander in Chief of the Texas army due to the military expertise he received from his fraternal brother, Andrew Jackson. Houston also became the first President of the Republic of Texas and had been Governor of Tennessee. Houston received his Masonic degrees in Cumberland Lodge No. 8 in Nashville. On 19 April 1817, Houston received his first glimpse of light in Masonry as an Entered Apprentice. On 20 June 1817, Houston received further light in Masonry by being passed to the degree of Fellow Craft, and on 22 July 1817, he was honored with the square and compasses by being raised to the sublime degree of a Master Mason. Houston was also an original member of the Grand Lodge of Texas, as well as the presiding officer of the convention[23]. After the victory at the Alamo, Santa Anna was convinced that the Texans had been defeated and that victory was his. Santa Anna divided his army and led the Mexican army to east Texas to return to Mexico by ship. His confidence in himself and in his army allowed the Texas army to take him by surprise. On the battlefield at San Jacinto on 21 April 1836, the Army of Texas commanded by General

Sam Houston accompanied by the Texas Secretary of War and member of Milam lodge No. 2, Thomas J. Rusk, attacked the larger invading army of Mexicans led by Santa Anna. At the Battle of San Jacinto, Santa Anna was captured by Sam Houston and his troops and the Mexican army was defeated. One presumptuous legend contends that Sam Houston spared Santa Anna's life because Santa Anna announced himself as a Mason to Houston. Even though many Texan soldiers demanded Santa Anna's execution, Sam Houston decided that Santa Anna was worth more alive than dead. On 14 May 1836, Santa Anna signed a peace treaty negotiated with the acting President of Texas and member of Holland Lodge No. 1, David G. Burnet, as well as other Texas officials. In the Treaty of Velasco Santa Anna promised to end the war and order all Mexican troops in Texas to retire to the south of the Rio Bravo. In a secret agreement, President Burnet promised to return Santa Anna safely to Mexico so he could encourage his government to adopt the treaty[24].

Tolerance has always been one of Freemasonry's virtues. From the earliest days of Speculative Masonry, political and religious disputes among Masons have been forbidden and the tenets of brotherly love, relief and truth have always been universally present in the Craft. One of the earliest famous incidents known of a Mason showing such sympathy to another is the case of Chief of the Mohawks, Joseph Brant and a young scout, Lt. Boyd. In 1779, General Sullivan, a Mason, ambushed the Indians and Loyalists in Newton, New York. During this ambush, a young Mason and scout for Sullivan named Lt. Boyd was captured along with a solider named Parker. Lt. Boyd was spared by Brant after identifying himself as a Mason. This incident happened as follows, according to John Salmon a friend of Boyd:

> When Lt. Boyd found himself a prisoner, he solicited an interview with Brant, whom he well

knew commanded the Indians. This chief, who was at that moment near, immediately presented himself, Lt. Boyd, by one of those appeals which are known only by those who have been initiated and instructed in certain mysteries, and which never fails to bring assistance to a "distressed brother", addressed him as the only source from which he could expect a respite from cruel punishment or death. The appeal was recognized, and Brant immediately, and in the strongest language, assured him that his life should be spared. Lt Boyd and his fellow-prisoner Parker were immediately conducted by a party of Indians to the Indian village called Beards Town.

Brant was the first Native American to be initiated into the Craft. He was made a Mason in London and was a member of lodge of Friendship No. 2.[24]

The United States was founded using Masonic principles and symbolism. No other nation was conceived or dedicated to the principles of Masonry and the tenets that its members followed before or since. The Square the Compasses and the United States go together just as "One nation under God" does. Both the *Pledge of Allegiance* and

the National Anthem were written by Freemasons. The

Reverend Francis J. Bellamy is known for writing the

pledge of allegiance. Bellamy was a Mason, a member of

Little Falls Lodge No. 181, located in Little Falls, New

York. Francis Scott Key wrote the *Star Spangled Banner*

during the war of 1812. Francis Scott Key was a member

of Columbia Lodge No. 31, along with his good friend

President James K. Polk.[25]

The Most Worshipful Grand Lodge of

Massachusetts states

The principles of Freemasonry, Brotherly
Love, Relief and Truth inspired the founders of this nation.
Today, we recognize these principles as the Cornerstones
of the American way of life. Early American Masons such
as George Washington, John Hancock, Paul Revere, Prince
Hall, Benjamin Franklin and many others were members of
the Brotherhood of Freemasons. Together they deliberately
incorporated Masonic principles into the most important
founding documents of this country. May they long endure,
for they are our true security.[26]

Freemasons have been a great influence in

American History and will be for years to come. It is

Freemasonry's use of symbolism that distinguishes it from the mundane and imperialistic symbolism of iconoclastic religious cultures and seals of regal powers that long established and then contributed to the rise and fall of nations of the Earth. These symbols were chosen to be incorporated into our nation's flags, currency and other important particulars, and yet, not one single undertaking is so clearly delineated or marked with that beneficent level of government, as is the Constitution of the United States. The influence of the Square and Compasses have been seen in several episodes of this country's history, as well as being a very powerful symbol in the nation's perpetual records. Symbols are given power by people: alone, a symbol is meaningless, but with enough people behind it, the belief in what a symbol in action stands for can change the course of history, and even the world. And so mote it ever be!

NOTES

[1] Pete Normand, *The Texas Mason; The Fraternity of Ancient Free & Accepted Masons in the History of Texas*, (Brazos Valley Masonic Library and Museum Assn., 1986), 5

[2] John Hamill and Robert Gilbert, ed *Freemasonry; A Celebration of the Craft*, (London.: Angus Books., 2004), 66, 113 –19, 164-65, 227

[3] Bernard E. Jones, *Freemasons' Guide and Compendium*, New and Revised ed. (Great Britain.: Eric Dobby Publishing Ltd., 1994),19 – 69.

[4] *Monitor of the Lodge, Grand Lodge of Texas A.F.& A. M.* (Waco, TX.: Waco Printing Co., 1982), 69

[5] Jasper Ridley, *The Freemasons; A History of the World's Most Powerful Secret Society* (New York.: Arcade Publishing, 2001),43

[6] Christopher Hodapp, *Freemasons for Dummies*, (Hoboken, NJ.: Wiley Publishing Inc., 2005), 38.

[7] Sachse, Julius F. *Masonic Correspondence of Washington as found among the Washington papers in the Library of Congress.* Grand Lodge of Pennsylvania, Philadelphia, 1915.

[8] James D. Carter, *Masonry in Texas; background, history, and influence to 1846*, 2nd ed. (Waco, TX.: Committee on Masonic Education and Service of the Grand Lodge of Texas, A.F. & A.M., 1958), 104

[9] Steven C, Bullock, *Revolutionary Brotherhood; Freemasonry and the Transformation of the American Social Order, 1730 – 1840*, (Williamsburg, VA.: Institute of Early American History and Culture, University North Carolina, 1996),85, Jasper Ridley, *The Freemasons; A History of the World's Most Powerful Secret Society* (New York.: Arcade Publishing, 2001),92, James D. Carter, *Masonry in Texas; background, history, and influence to 1846*, 2nd ed. (Waco, TX.: Committee on Masonic Education and Service of the Grand Lodge of Texas, A.F. & A.M., 1958), 78

[10] James D. Carter, *Masonry in Texas; background, history, and influence to 1846*, 2nd ed. (Waco, TX.: Committee on Masonic Education and Service of the Grand Lodge of Texas, A.F. & A.M., 1958),49, 57-58, Steven C, Bullock, *Revolutionary Brotherhood; Freemasonry and the Transformation of the American Social Order, 1730 – 1840*, (Williamsburg, VA.: Institute of Early American History and Culture, University North Carolina, 1996), 107, 111, 113, H. Paul H Jeffers, *Freemasons; A History and Exploration of the World's Oldest Secret Society,* (New York, NY.: Citadel Press Kensington Publishing Crop, 2005),43.

[11] James D. Carter, *Masonry in Texas; background, history, and influence to 1846*, 2nd ed. (Waco, TX.: Committee on Masonic

Education and Service of the Grand Lodge of Texas, A.F. & A.M., 1958),50-53, Steven C, Bullock, *Revolutionary Brotherhood; Freemasonry and the Transformation of the American Social Order, 1730 – 1840,* (Williamsburg, VA.: Institute of Early American History and Culture, University North Carolina, 1996), 96-97.

[12] Christopher Hodapp, *Freemasons for Dummies,* (Hoboken, NJ.: Wiley Publishing Inc., 2005), 38

[13] Steven C, Bullock, *Revolutionary Brotherhood; Freemasonry and the Transformation of the American Social Order, 1730 – 1840,* (Williamsburg, VA.: Institute of Early American History and Culture, University North Carolina, 1996),113, H. Paul H Jeffers, *Freemasons; A History and Exploration of the World's Oldest Secret Society,* (New York, NY.: Citadel Press Kensington Publishing Crop, 2005), 41-42, 53.

[14] James D. Carter, *Masonry in Texas; background, history, and influence to 1846,* 2nd ed. (Waco, TX.: Committee on Masonic Education and Service of the Grand Lodge of Texas, A.F. & A.M., 1958), 49, 50, Steven C, Bullock, *Revolutionary Brotherhood; Freemasonry and the Transformation of the American Social Order, 1730 – 1840,* (Williamsburg, VA.: Institute of Early American History and Culture, University North Carolina, 1996),107, 113.

[15] James D. Carter, *Masonry in Texas; background, history, and influence to 1846,* 2nd ed. (Waco, TX.: Committee on Masonic Education and Service of the Grand Lodge of Texas, A.F. & A.M., 1958),183, Jasper Ridley, *The Freemasons; A History of the World's Most Powerful Secret Society* (New York.: Arcade Publishing, 2001),151 –57.

[16] William F. Deverell and Anne F. Hyde, *The West: in the history of the nation* (Bedford / St. Martins, Boston, 2000), 222.

[17] James D. Carter, *Masonry in Texas; background, history, and influence to 1846,* 2nd ed. (Waco, TX.: Committee on Masonic Education and Service of the Grand Lodge of Texas, A.F. & A.M., 1985), 171

[18] James D. Carter, *Masonry in Texas; background, history, and influence to 1846,* 2nd ed. (Waco, TX.: Committee on Masonic Education and Service of the Grand Lodge of Texas, A.F. & A.M., 1985), 160, 270.

[19] James D. Carter, *Masonry in Texas; background, history, and influence to 1846,* 2nd ed. (Waco, TX.: Committee on Masonic Education and Service of the Grand Lodge of Texas, A.F. & A.M., 1985), 257 –58, Pete Normand, *The Texas Mason; The Fraternity of*

Ancient Free & Accepted Masons in the History of Texas, (Brazos
Valley Masonic Library and Museum Assn., 1986), 16.

[20] James D. Carter, *Masonry in Texas; background, history, and
influence to 1846,* 2nd ed. (Waco, TX.: Committee on Masonic
Education and Service of the Grand Lodge of Texas, A.F. & A.M.,
1985), 312-13.

[21] Cliff Cameron, "Ancient York Masons of San Felipe: A Historical
Presentation on the First Documented Masonic Meeting That Took
Place in Colonial Texas at San Felipe de Austin, February 11, 1828"
Paper Presented at Gray Lodge 329, October 2007, 4

[22] Determined by the plaque hanging on the south wall of the barracks
at the Alamo, which says – The birthplace of Freemasonry in West
Texas This plaque was dedicated... honoring those pioneer masons of
that era who founded a lodge upon this site.

[23] Pete Normand, *The Texas Mason; The Fraternity of Ancient Free &
Accepted Masons in the History of Texas,* (Brazos Valley Masonic
Library and Museum Assn., 1986), 8-10

[24] James D. Carter, *Masonry in Texas; background, history, and
influence to 1846,* 2nd ed. (Waco, TX.: Committee on Masonic
Education and Service of the Grand Lodge of Texas, A.F. & A.M.,
1985), 161-62, 270, 293, 313

[25] Pete Normand, *The Texas Mason; The Fraternity of Ancient Free &
Accepted Masons in the History of Texas,* (Brazos Valley Masonic
Library and Museum Assn., 1986), 13, 21

[26] John Hamill and Robert Gilbert, ed *Freemasonry; A Celebration of
the Craft,* (London.: Angus Books., 2004),204-05

[27] Archives from the Most Worshipful Grand Lodge of Maryland A. F.
& A. M. www.mdmasons.org/famous.html

[28] Archives from the Most Worshipful Grand Lodge of Massachusetts.
A.F. & A. M.

Chapter Two
THE TRUE MASONIC EXPERIENCE

"Masonic labor is to learn - and to teach others."

These were some of the first words ever spoken to me by a

man I greatly admire – and they changed my world forever.

Why? Well we will get to that, but first let me ask you a

question. How was your last or most recent masonic

experience? Was it what you pictured Freemasonry would

be when you first petitioned the lodge? If you answered

yes, well then you are part of lucky few whose actual

expectations were met. However, if you are like the rest of

us, you have conformed your thinking and have accepted

the most recent practices as what Freemasonry has always

been. Now, by saying this I am not trying to insult your lodge or any of your Masonic experiences. My job today is not to get you to like me, or even get you to agree with me. My job is to make you think, to make you question your masonic experience, and to see if your actual expectations from this fraternity have been met. Not only that but it is my hope that I can help you enhance the experience that you are undergoing at your local lodge.

There are two groups of people that are essential in every lodge, the Past Masters and the new members. These members are an asset to the lodge, but not for reasons most people would think. Past Masters are the history and keepers of the lodge. They are the holders of the traditions, the allegories, and the teachers. They are the ones that can carry the lodge on for generations, or the ones that can damage it to the point of disrepair. They are the ones who can and will pass on their good and bad habits to future generations of Freemasons. The new candidates are the lifeline of the organization. They are the ones that will receive the information from the Past Masters, absorb it, become officers and repeat the cycle. If a lodge continues to introduce bad habits, and dilutes the experience, then it is not long before the original intent of the experience is gone.

The lessons of Freemasonry are impeccable, and almost everything put in its allegories is there for a reason. Therefore, as a craftsman in search of light, one should always question everything in order to truly understand and apprehend the lessons. How else is the apprentice, supposed to apply the teachings of the craft to his life, and become a better man in the process, if he does not understand what he is being told? Furthermore, how are teachers supposed to instruct if they are not completely certain of the answer? Let us use your initiation as the example.

You Will Await the Time with Patience

What is the first command you are given when you are initiated into the fraternity? Go back and think of your own initiation, and try to remember what command you were given when you knocked at the inner door of the lodge. You were told to await the time with patience. Have you ever wondered why that is the first command you are ever given when beginning your Masonic Journey? In this fast-paced world we live in today; Freemasonry gives you the opportunity to slow things down. Freemasonry was designed to do just that – we are taught that with time, patience, and perseverance we may overcome all things. A man should not petition a lodge in January and become a 32nd degree Scottish Rite Mason by the end of the summer. The lessons of Freemasonry take a lifetime to study, yet alone understand. Lodges, Masonic Organizations and individuals should never be in too big a hurry to advance through the lessons and allegories that Freemasonry offers.

When one travels to foreign Masonic Jurisdictions, especially outside of the United States, one will find the advancement of Freemasonry is much different from the one we experience here in the United States. It takes years to become a Master Mason in most jurisdictions, and to advance beyond that could even be decades. As an example, let us compare the legal requirements from my home Jurisdiction – The Grand Lodge of Texas, to that of the Grand Lodge of Denmark of the Swedish Rite.

In the Grand Lodge of Texas, a petitioner files a petition with the lodge he wishes to join. That petition is read at the next stated meeting. The Worshipful Master appoints a committee of three Master Masons to "investigate the candidate" and report at the subsequent stated meeting. The committee may take whichever legal liberty they like to satisfy themselves of that petitioner. The committee is encouraged to visit with the petitioner at his home, meet his wife and family, and explain to them what his masonic journey will entail. However, in most cases, this is not what happens. In my experience, I was invited to a very noisy restaurant where four men asked me a few question that were on a sheet they were provided. By the end, the Chairman of the investigating committee told me I would make an excellent Mason. My petition was balloted on the very next day, and I was elected to receive the degrees. At the time, those men did not really know anything about me. Yet they were satisfied that I would make an excellent Mason because I answered a few simple questions they were provided by the Grand Lodge. The investigation process to the candidate's initiation can take as little as a month.

From there the candidate is initiated after paying a small initiation fee, I paid $60 for my Entered Apprentice degree. According to Grand Lodge Law, an Entered Apprentice Mason must wait 30 days and learn 74 answers to a series of trial questions before being advanced to the next degree. Which I did, and a very short time later, I was passed to the degree of Fellowcraft. I paid a small $50 degree fee to receive the Fellowcraft degree. I was also informed that I had to learn the answer to 37 trial questions, and wait 15 days before I can receive my Master's degree. All of which I did, and shortly thereafter I was raised to the Sublime degree of a Master Mason. I paid $125 to receive that degree, which included the prorated dues for the rest of the year. After the degree, I was told that I had to learn the answer to 34 trial questions to which I had a year to do it in, and could not join any other Masonic bodies until I did. This I energetically undertook and stood for my examination the following week. After doing so, I was told that I could buy a life membership to the lodge for $500 and I was given a petition to the Scottish Rite. I purchased said life membership and petition the Scottish Rite immediately. I paid $875 to join the Scottish Rite as a life member and I became a 32nd degree Mason. I was also given a petition for the York Rite, and joined as a life member for a total of $1,000 just a few months later. Now all within a year I joined the fraternity, was raised to the Sublime Degree of a Master Mason, became a 32nd degree Scottish Rite Mason, and Knighted as a Knight Templar. Not only that, but the grand total for all of my degree fees as well as a life membership for all those bodies was $2,610. Now that might seem like a lot of money, but I joined at 21 years old and I never have to pay dues to any of those organizations ever again. On the other hand, the process in Swedish Rite in Denmark is much different. After a very rigorous investigation, and the candidate professing that he is a Christian who has been baptized, he may be invited to be initiated. The initiation fee for the first degree has a minimum degree fee set at $300, and 1-year attendance requirement to advance to the second degree. That is 1 year of attending and participating, not just being a card-carrying member. Once the candidate has been elected to advance to the second degree, he has to pay another $300 degree fee and attend another full year. The tableau below illustrates the advancement in the Swedish Rite a little better.

Time Spent in Degrees and Requirements for the Swedish Rite.

- I to II grade – 1 year as a I grade, attendance requirements, and a minimum of a $300 degree fee.
- II to III grade – 1 year as an II grade, attendance requirements, and a minimum of a $300 degree fee.
- III to IV/ V grade – 1 year as a III grade, attendance requirements, and a minimum of a $300 degree fee.
- IV / V to VI grade - 1 year and a half as a IV / V grade, attendance requirements, and a minimum of a $300 degree fee.
- VI to VII grade – 2 years as a VI grade, attendance requirements, and a minimum of a $300 degree fee.
- VII to VIII grade – 2 and a half years as a VII and a minimum of a $700 degree fee and a coat of arms.
- VIII to IX grade – 4 years as a VIII grade and a $700 degree fee
- IX to X grade – 7 years as a IX grade and a $1,500 degree fee.

Now that is a minimum of 20 years and $4,400 in just degree fees, not counting dues. The Scottish Rite and Swedish Rite are in amnesty and have a degree equivalence, therefore a 32nd degree Scottish Rite Mason is that equivalent to a VIII grade in the Swedish Rite. When you compare these two experiences, within 365 days I became a life member and a 32 degree Mason for the sum of $1,600. While in Denmark, a Mason would take nine (9) full years of participating, learning, and at least $2,200 in just degree fees, not to mention his annual dues to get to the same place.

Why is it like that here in the United States? Why does it only take such a short time for a Mason to attain such a high degree, when it was intended to take a lifetime to experience this? We are cheapening the experience of our members by trying to speed up this process. Freemasonry is first and foremost a learning institution. We are focusing too much on the aspect of Quantity instead of

Quality. We have created a generation of dues card-carrying members, instead of Masons learning their craft.

In the November / December 2012 issue of the Scottish Rite Journal, Ronald A. Seale 33°, Grand Commander of Southern Jurisdiction of Ancient and Accepted Scottish Rite Masonry stated his frustration with this process as follows: "We don't give our candidates time to absorb and assimilate the profound truths and right living that undergirds all that we do and are. We're in a hurry, they're in a hurry, and something is lost in the process." However most jurisdictions have made no real effort to address this situation. We need to remember the first command we are given when we knock upon the door of our lodges and apply it. We need to accept and submit to those instructions and await the time with patience, and actually absorb the lessons we are taught from our several masonic degrees.

The Candidate

Everything we do should be about the Candidate, from the rituals, degrees, lessons etc. When we are conferring a degree upon a new candidate, that entire experience should be for him. The degree should never be conferred to please the Committee on Work or Grand Lecturers, the Grand Lodge, Past Masters of the lodge, or even Grand Masters. It all should be for the candidate. The initiation experience of the candidate should never be cheapened for the sake of doing the degree "perfectly". The ritual must be memorized and memorized accurately. However, while performing the ritual, if you mess up your part, do not apologize. Pick up and keep going with the ceremony. Saying "I am sorry" and apologizing when one makes a mistake is not Freemasonry. You have to meet the candidate's expectations. The candidate does not know you made a mistake; therefore, you should not point that out to him. You have to give them Light – that is what they asked for. That is the only way a man becomes a Mason.

They say Masonry makes a good man better, but what part of the ritual does that? Because you can parrot back some ritual and make due-guards and secret signs with your hands? Does that make you a better man? Absolutely not! It is not until the candidate can understand the lessons behind that allegory that he can begin to become a better man. As we proceed through the degrees, we are asked specific questions. What came you here to do? The answer throughout Freemasonry is always the same, the words may be a little different in every jurisdiction, but the meaning is always the same. You came here to learn, you came here to subdue your passions, and to improve yourself in Masonry. As the candidate advances through the degrees, he is asked if he is a Fellowcraft Mason, and then if he is a Master Mason. The answer to the first question should be answer by saying "I am" then bashfully followed by searching for affirmation by challenging the person asking the question to "try me". By the time the candidate reaches the Sublime Degree of a Master Mason, he answers that same question by saying "I am" with no confirmation or clarification needed. Why is that? Have you ever wondered why the Master Mason is so confident? Think about that for a second.

We are Masons for ourselves, not to impress the public or the uninitiated. Every Masonic Ritual out there was created to teach or illustrate a lesson to the initiate. By trying to cut out certain aspects of the ritual, and watering it down, we are doing an injustice to those who knock on the doors of our lodges in search of light. A perfect example is the Grand Lodge of Massachusetts. That Grand Lodge has taken all of the penalties out of the obligations, and have replaced it with essentially saying, "you should feel bad". This was done because the penalties could be considered scary to the public.

American Timeline

Freemasonry is incapable of being improved; however, lodges themselves are not. Several lodges, Grand Lodges, and even appendant Masonic Bodies have had to adapt to certain situations in order to survive with changing times. Several Lodges in the United States have gotten away from our most sacred and valuable traditions. But why? In order to understand this we must first briefly explore the evolution of Freemasonry in this country.

In the 1640's is where we can find the first records of Scottish Operative Masons beginning to accept gentlemen Masons into their lodges. This is where we see the first transition from Operative Freemasonry to Speculative Freemasonry. By the year 1717, we see the beginning of the first Grand Lodge, The Grand Lodge of England, known then as the Grand Lodge of London and Westminster. The formation meeting of this new Grand Lodge took place at the Goose and Gridiron tavern in

London where four lodges met together to form the first Grand Lodge for two reasons. Frist to have a governing body to rule and govern over the aspects of Speculative Freemasonry. Second was to have an opportunity for these lodges to unite and observe the Feasts of the Holy St's John at Table.

By the year 1725, we see the first records of a Master Masons degree being conferred. In 1733, we see the formation of the first Masonic Lodge in the United States, St. John's Lodge in Boston, Massachusetts. As our fight for Independence from England was taking place, Masonic Lodges began declaring their independent from European Grand Lodges in 1776. By 1803, the mainstream independent American Grand Lodges we know today were established. Much like today, many Masons were in search of more light. There were several Masonic degrees being conferred at the time that were considered "higher degrees", but it was not until 1798 that we see those higher degrees start to become organized.

In 1798, the General Grand Chapter of Royal Arch Masons was formed in New York. Only 3 years later, the Supreme Council Southern Jurisdiction of the Ancient and Accepted Scottish Rite was formed in 1801 in Charleston, South Carolina, with the Northern Jurisdiction to follow in 1813. Finally, the Grand Encampment of Knight Templar of the United States was formed in New York in 1816. Masonry continued to grow well into the 19th century, however there were several challenges along the way.

Freemasonry's biggest hurdle occurred in the 1820's due to a man named Captain William Morgan, in an episode referred to as the Morgan Affair. In 1826, William Morgan disappeared after threatening to publish Masonic Secrets in an expose. Morgan was arrested for an outstanding debt. He disappeared soon after, and was believed to have been kidnapped and killed by Masons from western New York. Morgan was never heard from again, and his disappearance sparked an Anti-Masonic outcry throughout the country. To such a great extent that the Anti-Masonic political party was created as a third party who opposed Freemasonry as the most important issue. In the election of 1832, the Anti-Masonic Party ran William Wirt against the sitting President Andrew Jackson, a Freemason and Past Grand Master of Tennessee. Jackson won the presidency, but the movement did take a toll on Freemasonry as a whole. Major Grand Lodges like the Grand Lodge of Massachusetts, and the Grand Lodge of New York had to close over half of their Lodges. While the Grand Lodge of Vermont closed its doors completely. This caused Freemasonry to evolve, and most Grand Lodges who had an invitational requirement to join the fraternity were forced to change into a more transparent one. The exclusivity and secrecy of the organization diminished, and the revolving door mentality of attaining membership became the norm, and mottos like 2B1Ask1 were created. The rituals of Freemasonry began to be watered down and the "scarier" aspects of the rituals were passed on to the "higher degrees" in an attempt to appease the public.

By the 1850's a movement of women wanting to become Masons became prominent. However, since one of the landmarks of Freemasonry is that only men can be Freemasons, no regular Grand Lodge could initiate women and remain regular. Masonry once again evolved in order to satisfy this growing trend. In 1850, Rob Morris wrote and created a set of the degrees known as the Order of Eastern Star that conferred its rituals on Master Masons, their wives, mothers, sisters, and daughters. In 1873, a similar order called the Order of Amaranth was created and in 1894, the White Shrine of Jerusalem was created. These organizations satisfied that need of women being part of the Fraternity and once again, Masonry evolved to satisfy the public.

From 1870 through the 1920's is an era known as the "Fraternal Period". Many people during this time wanted something to belong to, and several social fraternal organizations like Greek fraternities and social groups like the Elks lodge or Moose lodges began showing up. Many Masons wanted a similar experience, and wanted a place where they could get away from the more structured part of Freemasonry to a more relaxed atmosphere. In 1870, many Masons in Manhattan discussed the idea of a Fraternity of Masons stressing fun and fellowship. Walter Fleming and William Florence took this idea into fruition and after a trip to Egypt formed the Arabic Order of the Nobles of the Mystic Shrine (A.A.O.N.M.S.) and by 1872 the Shrine as we know it today was born. Many other social Masonic Groups sprouted during this time. In 1889 the Mystic Order of Veiled Prophets of the Enchanted Realm, also known as the Grotto was formed in New York. By 1902, a similar order known as the Tall Cedars of Lebanon was created. In

1905, an organization called the Scoits was created with the purpose of having a social group to encourage Masons to become more active in their Lodges by participating in social activities. In 1917, the National Sojourners was created as a way to have Masons who served in the armed forces, participate in a social organization of likeminded individuals. By 1921, the High Twelve Club was formed as a lunch club for Masons. Thus, during this period of fraternalism, Freemasonry evolved once again in order to satisfy this movement in American history.

As we moved into the 20th century Masons wanted to involve their families into their Masonic activities. As a way to introduce or explain why dad was away at lodge, without giving away any of the secrets, the youth groups were born. The Order of DeMolay being the first one, established in 1919 as an organization for boys to learn the social and structural attributes needed to be a successful member of society. This was followed with the Job's

Daughters in 1920 and the Order of Rainbow for girls in 1922.

As mentioned earlier, Masonry passed on some of their more esoteric rituals and traditions to higher degrees. In order to keep some of these mysteries, invitational degrees started springing up in an attempt to keep these traditions alive.

The Red Cross of Constantine was brought to the United States in 1870 as an invitational body for those who belong to the Chapter of Royal Arch Masons. This organization is now restricted to forty-five (45) per Conclave (lodge) and the number of Conclaves is limited per number of Royal Arch Masons in a geographical location.

The Royal order of Scotland was the next to be brought to the United Sates in 1877. This invitational body confers two degrees upon members who are 32nd degree

Scottish Rite Masons or Knights Templar, who have been a Master Mason at least 5 years. The Provincial Grand Lodge confers the degrees a few times a year in various places around the United States.

In 1886, the Societas Rosicruciana in Civitatibus Foederatis, or SRICF was established in the United States. It is an esoteric Rosicrucian Society composed of Master Masons, limited to 72 members per college. Typically, each state only has one College, with a few exceptions. Those being Texas, New York and California.

The Knight Beneficent of the Holy City also known as the C.B.C.S is the most exclusive and esoteric of them all. This organization was brought to the United States in 1928, and is limited to 72 members per prefecture. Until very recently that meant that only one or two members per state could be initiated nationally.

In the 1930's a man names John Raymond Shute brought or created a number of Invitational bodies into the United States. In 1930, the KYCH or Knight York Cross of Honor was created as a way to honor Masons who have presided over a Lodge of Masons, a Chapter of Royal Arch Masons, a Council of Royal and Select Masters, and a Commandery of Knights Templar.

 In 1931, the Order of Holy Royal Arch Knight Templar Priest or HRAKTP was established in the US as an invitational body for Past Commanders of a Commandery of Knights Templar, who have served with great distinction. Thirty-three (33) members can be initiated into a Tabernacle and the number of Tabernacles is predicated on the number of Commanderies or Priories in a geographical area.

 The Allied Masonic Degrees was established in the United States in 1932, as an organization, which encompasses several Masonic Rites. It confers several degrees in a non-ascending order. Membership is limited to 27 members per Council, limited to those who are Royal Arch Masons.

The Society of Blue Friars was also established in 1932 as an organization of scholars composed of those who have contributed largely to Masonic research.

The Knight Masons of Ireland was brought to the United States in 1936; it confers 3 degrees to Masons who are Royal Arch Masons.

Lastly, the Sovereign York Rite College of North America was formed in 1957 as a way to honor those who are active in their Lodge, Chapter, Council and Commandery.

These invitational bodies are the only Masonic Organizations where a person may not petition to receive the degrees, but rather must be invited. In most cases if the Mason askes to join he will never be rendered an invitation.

These organizations are some of the last remaining places where a Mason must prove himself, in order to attain the light provided within its teachings and precepts.

Masonic Restoration

So what is the biggest problem with Freemasonry today? Well there may be several, but the most prominent one is that we are not giving our candidates what we promise them. We are promising them a great fraternity, that teaches a man how to become a better person by a system of morality and allegories that will improve his life. We are selling them the Craft of Benjamin Franklin, George Washington and Paul Revere. However, what we are giving them is spaghetti on paper plates, pancake breakfasts and arguing over the utility bills. We are not giving candidates Masonry anymore. Freemasonry is not a pancake breakfast and spaghetti dinners. It is not fundraisers, and programs on how to write your will, or how to check your prostate. It is not paying the bills and discussing what wattage lightbulbs we need in the kitchen. If you give your candidates what they asked for, they will gladly pay for it.

Masonry is no longer a distinguished institution. It has become uninspired and hollow. But how do we get back to being so, how do we fix this? That answer is simple, through Masonic Restoration. Observing and bringing back the original principles of our Fraternity is the best way to restore American Freemasonry to its original glory. We are Masons for ourselves, and not to impress the public. Key parts of the Freemasonry should not be omitted because it may scare, or confuse the un-initiated. So what are some of those ancient and honorable traditions? Well one of those has already been mentioned as one of the reasons the first Grand Lodge was created. When Freemasonry started, they did not have the extravagant buildings and Masonic Temples we have today. Masons originally convened at pubs and taverns and conducted their meetings around the table, in what is called a Table Lodge. Today however, mentioning alcohol in a lodge may get you in trouble. Another ancient tradition that has been lost to most American Masons is that of the Chamber of Reflection. This Chamber was a tool to the ritual intended to make the candidate ask himself – "what came you here to do?" Yet, most masons have never heard of this. Both of these traditions have their own chapter so I will not go too deep into them here.

Another very important aspect of improving the experience of your members is the lodge attire. Every Mason should attend Lodge "properly clad for noble deeds, higher thoughts, and greater achievements." Your dress is the first impression of your lodge; your attire should show your commitment to the craft. When attending lodge, you should always attend with the attire that shows true respect to this time honored institution. In most jurisdictions around the world, Masons are required to attend lodge in a black suit and tie or Tuxedo. If a Mason, even a visitor, is not properly dressed, he will not be allowed in. This seems to be a touchy subject in some lodges around this country, but it is one we all need to understand. The most common opposing argument to this is that "it is the internal not the external qualifications that recommend a man to be made a Mason". That may be, but key word there being recommend. That means that Masonry, nor its members will not judge you for what you do for a living – we are all on the level. That does not mean that it should tolerate a Mason disrespecting the institution, by attending lodge in a tank top, shorts and flip-flops.

Every Mason should attend lodge, dressed as they would dress to attend an important event in their life. Such as a friend's is wedding, a child christening or even a graduation. I belong to St. Alban's Lodge No. 1455, in College Station, TX. We have a dress code at this lodge that all members shall wear a tuxedo, white shirt, and black bow-tie to all meetings of the lodge. This dress code has made other lodges in the area think of St Alban's as being an elitist or arrogant lodge. However, this could not be further from the truth. We selected the Tuxedo as our uniform for two reasons. One, a tuxedo shows true respect that we as members have towards our lodge and our fraternity. Two, and most importantly, a tuxedo puts every man on the level. If a Mason visits our lodge, they cannot tell who the millionaire is, and who starving college student is. Why? Because everyone is dressed the same. Granted the millionaire might be wearing a two thousand dollar Armani Tuxedo, while the college student is wearing a used tuxedo he purchased from the sale bin for $50. However, you would never tell just by looking at it. If those two same Masons attend a lodge, while the millionaire is wearing a two thousand dollar Armani suit, and the college student is wearing a t-shirt, flip-flops and cargo shorts, well are they really on the level?

Another aspect of being properly clad does not just stop at your attire, but your apron as well. Are you wearing your apron with equal pleasure to yourself and honor to the fraternity? Is the cloth apron that is provided to you outside the door of the lodge, the best representation of this statement? It should not be, furthermore, if you attend a lodge in a jurisdiction outside of the United States and do not have your own apron, it is likely they will not have one for you to wear. Therefore, you will not be allowed admittance. It is not the lodge's responsibility to provide you with an apron. That responsibility is for you and you alone. There are several apron manufactures out there that can provide you with a quality apron that you can be proud of, and attend lodge properly clad.

Masonry is Magic – it is filled with mystery, and when we allow ourselves to let the profane and un-initiated to know our mysteries, our secrets, and why we have a letter G over the East, we become the magician that shows the audience how he cut the woman in half. There is a reason why we use words like "Temple", "profane" and "conclave". The word conclave is a word that derives from the Latin phrase *Con Clave,* which was an assembly or gathering for only those who were worthy or had special authority to be there. The phrase *Con Clave* literally translates to "under lock and key". The word *profane* is an even better example. Profane comes from the Latin *pro,* meaning "before" and *Janum* meaning "a temple." Hence, in Masonry it means those who have not been in the Temple. In other words, they have not been initiated so they should not know that a lodge room looks like. The public and uninitiated were never meant to be in our Temples, lodge rooms or ceremonial places. The magic in Freemasonry is special because we as Masons have it, and others do not.

Masonic Principles of Traditional Masonry

Every lodge should aspire to see that they are seen in the eyes of Masonry as a "Vanguard Lodge". According to John M. Hilliard, Past Master of Independent Royal Arch Lodge No. 2 in New York City, there are 7 principles a lodge should follow in order to be considered a valuable Masonic lodge in the eyes of the world. They are as follows:

7 Principles of Traditional Masonry

1) RITUAL EXCELLENCE: This principle demands that the ritual be completely and artistically rendered from memory. This is the single most fundamental element of traditional Freemasonry. This includes the requirement that every man learn the lectures through the trial questions and answers of each degree.

2) EDUCATION: This principle demands that a regular program of education and indoctrination be followed grounding the membership in the rich and complex history, literature, culture and traditions of the craft of Freemasonry.

3) THE TABLE LODGE (or Festive Board): This tradition is indispensable as nothing can replace the experience of Freemasons sitting down together to a meal, presided over by the Worshipful Master and Wardens, where conviviality and the traditions of the lodge and the fraternity can be observed and preserved. (The Table Lodge stands in direct contrast to the increasingly more common practice of serving a meager meal of spaghetti, sandwiches, or barbecue on paper plates before or after the monthly meeting.)

4) CHARITABLE OUTREACH: The lodge should have an ongoing program of charitable outreach to the immediate community. The charitable program of the lodge should be provided for separate and apart from the lodge treasury and its annual budget.

5) ELEGANCE OF DRESS: This should preferably include black tie (or dark suit) at all regular meetings, degree conferrals, and festive boards of the lodge. A Freemason's dress for lodge meetings should exhibit the same respect for his lodge and his fellows as he would exhibit when attending a friend's wedding, a child's christening, a nephew's graduation, or any other significant event. This principle also includes other regalia, accoutrements, and surroundings as best as the lodge resources can muster. A lodge should be well kept and in good repair outside and well-furnished and decorated, neat

and clean on the inside.

6) SELECTIVITY AND EXCLUSIVITY: A scrupulous screening of candidates and affiliates insures that only the most excellent of men, superior in character, ability, honesty, and potential are admitted. Compatibility with the membership is an important characteristic to consider. Balloting on affiliations should ALWAYS be done by secret ballot.

7) COMMITMENT: A demand for a real sacrifice of time, talent, and means from those who seek to exercise leadership in the lodge is indispensable. A commensurate commitment from those members who only wish to sit on the sidelines is also important.

3 Additional Principles of Traditional Masonry

According to Pierre G. "Pete" Normand Jr., Past Master of St Alban's Lodge No. 1455 in College Station, TX, there are three more principles that should be added to this. They are as follows:

8) DECORUM DURING MEETINGS: Observing a special decorum during meetings of the Lodge is probably the single most important point of traditional Freemasonry. By streamlining the regular business of the Lodge, and limiting the length of meetings to one hour, more time is allowed for the Festive Board, after-proceedings and fellowship. Minutes of previous meetings are never read aloud, but are made available to the membership before the meeting, giving them the opportunity to offer corrections, so the minutes can be quickly approved by the Worshipful Master. Business brought before the Lodge is sent to a committee for study and a recommendation that can be easily and quickly approved by the membership at a later date. Meetings are never allowed to become simply a committee of the whole.

In addition to these more obvious aspects of efficiently conducting lodge business, the meetings of the Lodge should be conducted in a solemn and dignified manner with a minimum of distractions. The ritual should be as close to perfect as practice will produce. The ritual movement of the Deacons and other officers about the room should be measured, deliberate and precise. A darkened lodge room illuminated by beeswax candles helps to hide any visual distractions. A hint of incense eliminates musty smells and other distracting odors. Carefully chosen music eliminates unnecessary chatter, and focuses the members' attention on the ceremonies before them.

9) HIGHER INITIATION AND DINNING FEES:
Initiation fees are set at about five times the local norm. Dining fees are set high enough to allow the Lodge to hold its Festive Boards at the finest restaurants or country clubs in town, in order to provide a higher quality Masonic

dining experience for its members and new initiates. Endowed Membership fees are set at twenty-five times the amount of our annual dues.

10) SOCIAL EVENTS: Social events are important to the life of the Lodge. But social events where non-Masons are present are kept purely social, and never include Masonic speeches, long introductions or other Masonic programs. By the same token, when the Lodge conducts any kind of Masonic business (a Masonic speech, lecture or program, or any other Masonic business, to include the annual installation of officers) the profane are never included. As a result, the Lodge has never held an open installation of officers, and this is a rule that has been heartily endorsed by the wives of our members.

The Quadrant

In all aspects of our ritual, we are immersed with the notion of "whence we came". Nevertheless, we as Freemasons, not only need to focus on where we came from, but also in which direction we are heading. Through numerous studies done in several Masonic jurisdictions around the country there is one evident fact. Masonry has been on a decline for years! Several Grand Jurisdictions around the country have done many different things to fix the problem. Some have created a one-day "Festival" where Master Masons are made in a day by witnessing all 3 degrees. Some have shortened the memory work and time limitations needed to advance from degree to degree, some jurisdictions eliminating this process completely. One Grand Jurisdiction has even gone as far as "making Masons at sight" in mass stadium style "conferrals". Even worse, one Grand Lodge has created an incentive program, where a Mason can exchange degree petitions he submitted for consumer goods, such as a new set or luggage or a new set of golf clubs. But has this fixed the problem in those Grand Lodges? Have the tenets of Freemasonry been acquired and applied? Have they made good men better? Have they achieved their goal? Or have they diluted the process and just generated numbers to meet their needs and created a generation of dues card carrying Freemasons? That is for you to decide. Now that the thought is fresh on your mind, ask yourself this question; why did you join the Fraternity?

People join Freemasonry for many different reasons, but they remain an active member for only four reasons; Ritual, Masonic Light, Philanthropy, Fraternity. In our fraternity, you can place any active Mason into one of these four categories. Some might spill over into more than one or even all four, but if a lodge does not offer all four qualities, that lodge will not grow.

Allow me to break this down. Imagine you have a person (let us call him John) who is all about helping his community and being around people he likes / like minded people. Now John joins Ritual Lodge No. 7 because it happens to be the lodge closest to his house. Ritual Lodge No. 7 is composed of Masons who are all about ritualistic excellence, they practice the ritual once a week, they are extremely persistent about every aspect of the ritual, and only do degrees if they are being graded by the Committee on Work or a Grand Lecturer. John wanted to become a Mason because all of the men in his family have been Masons, but he does not share the views of Ritual Lodge No. 7, he is not really concerned about ritual. Now do you think John will be very active with this lodge once he is a Master Mason, if he even makes it through? Now picture John joining Shrine Lodge No. 4, where they do the ritual because they have to. However, one night a week the members of the lodge all get together for a social outing, and once a month they volunteer at the local Shrine Hospital. Where do you see John spending most of his

87

time? If John is not aware of Shrine Lodge, and he only experiences Ritual Lodge, the odds of him staying active, or even a member, are not very good.

Now let us break down the four categories:

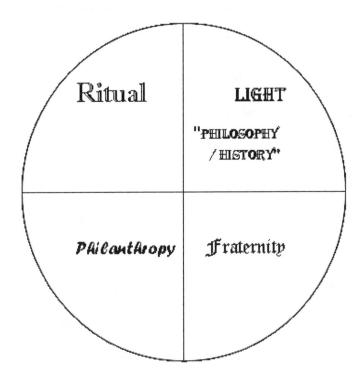

Ritual - The Ritualistic Mason is someone who really enjoys the rituals of the craft. They might enjoy watching degrees, conferring or doing different parts in the degrees. They might like studying the degrees and want to know where they came from. They might like joining different Masonic bodies and receiving "more light". They might just enjoy collecting degrees. A good example of a famous Mason of this kind would be Albert Pike - Past Sovereign Grand Commander of the Scottish Rite.

Light - The Philosophic / Historic Mason is someone who enjoys the history or philosophy of the craft. This can include those who have become Masons through history. How Masonry influenced different episodes in history. Studying where Freemasonry came from and how it evolved. Studying the philosophy, history, alchemy, psychology, or even spirituality of the craft. This is a student of Masonry, who is in search of Masonic Light. This may also include Masons who enjoy giving or hearing lectures, etc. A good example of this kind of Mason would be any Masonic author - such as Brent Morris, Arturo de Hoyos, or Rex Hutchens.

Philanthropy - The Philanthropic Mason is someone who enjoys the charity aspect of our craft. Whether it is helping a brother in need, or volunteering his time for a specific purpose. This could be someone who wants to help in the community by different means such as; collecting and distributing clothes and food for the needy, serving the teachers of the local school breakfast, giving scholarships, or planting trees. Creating endowment funds for charitable events, or even creating a string of hospitals like the Shrine did. A good example of this is illustrated by the Shriner's motto - "No man has ever stood so tall as when he stooped down to help a child."

Fraternity - The Fraternal Mason is someone who enjoys the fraternal aspect of the craft. This is the kind of Mason that enjoys any sort of gathering, Table Lodge's, lodge outings, picnics, family functions. Most officers of all Masonic organizations fall into this category, not because they only show up to be with people - but because as leaders the need to be "politically correct", friendly, and somewhat charismatic, and some might just have to politic and shake hands and kiss babies. Fraternal Masons may also enjoy going to the "Grand Functions" such as Grand Lodge, Supreme Council, Grand Encampment, or Masonic Week, this might be the one time a year they might see those friends from other areas.

Now think about the four categories for a minute and see where you land on our quadrant. Which quadrant or quadrants do you fall into? Does your Masonic experience meet your expectations? Are you active in your local Masonic organizations? If you answered yes to the last question, it is probably because your expectations where met, and you enjoy Masonry because your quadrant is being applied in your Lodge. However, the question now becomes "What if the answer was No?" How do we fix this?

Believe it or not the answer to that is simple. The one thing that every member has in common is that they are all Masons. From the youngest Entered Apprentice in the North East Corner, to the Worshipful Master of the lodge, they are all Masons. Masonry interests every Mason, which is why he joined the fraternity. If he had no interest in Masonry he would not have joined. So make sure that you do Masonry in your Lodge. Every Lodge must educate their members; after all, it is what they most desire – light! A good Lodge should have a program of some sort at every meeting. But make sure the program will interest all members of your Lodge. Most importantly make sure that all programs are of a Masonic nature. If you have a program about how to check your prostate, or how to write a will, your younger members will lose interest. On the other hand, if you have a program on the most up to date social media trends, your older members will lose interest. However, if you have a program on the hidden mysteries of Freemasonry - that will captivate most of your audience. No man should ever leave a Masonic meeting without learning something new.

Now it becomes your part to see if this is something you or your lodge is willing to take on, and help this great institution restore itself. It takes more than being there and saying you are going to do something to make the change. It takes dedication, it takes commitment, and it takes a drive. Many of our forgotten Masonic Traditions have been taken out of Freemasonry as a way to appease the un-initiated and the profane. These traditions like the Chamber of Reflection, should be performed in all regular Masonic Lodges. Not because it is cool, but because it is the right thing to do – because it is part of the True Masonic Experience.

Understanding all of this and knowing when someone asks you the question' "are you a Master Mason?' you can answer them confidently. You can do this because you know why you are a Master Mason, because you know the Masters' secrets, and because you do not share them with the profane. You should always be a good custodian of the mysteries that way you can "keep sacred and inviolable the mysteries of the Order, as these are to distinguish you from the rest of the community, and mark your consequence among Masons."

Chapter Three
THE TABLE LODGE: A FORGOTTEN MASONIC PRACTICE

We as Masons are very proud of our fraternity and its heritage. We are proud of our rites, our ritual, our traditions, and heaven forbid that anyone try and change something. We always hear "that's the way we have done it since time immemorial, and we are never going to change it." Still, it surprises me to learn that many Past Masters and other knowledgeable Masons have never heard of a Table Lodge. Almost all American Masons know about what some call the "knife and fork degree," in which the members of the lodge mingle about the dining room for the social hour of the lodge during refreshment. This tradition is typical in most American lodges where brethren usually share a meal before their meeting in a cafeteria-style fashion. These lodges invite families and non-Masons to the meal; the meal is usually mass produced style cuisine such as spaghetti, stew, barbeque, or chili. But what happened to the Table Lodge, the festive board, the Feasts of St's John? In a few places in the nation the old custom of the Table Lodge is still observed. But of the Masonic Feast as it was in the pre-Grand Lodge era and for many years after in England, we know very little.

The Table Lodge is one of the oldest Masonic traditions. The modern practice of Masonry was first perfected in the taverns and inns of Scotland and England, where early Lodges met and celebrated the social virtues of the Craft at the table. According to Henry Coil, "The Table Lodge was so common in the early 18th Century that it may be presumed that most meetings were of that character." Anciently, Masonic lodges convened at pubs, eateries or taverns since they did not have the luxury of extravagant buildings as we do today. The brethren would usually assemble at a local establishment on a night when there was a full moon. The full moon provided the most amount of light possible, essential since streets were lit by candles. Twice a year, Masons would gather in what is known as a Table Lodge, once in June and once in December. The Table Lodges were considered the two most important meetings of the year, because they were held to commemorate the Holy Saints John: St. John the Baptist in June and St. John the Evangelist in December. Both are also known as the Feasts of St John. According to the Book of Constitutions of the Mother Grand Lodge in 1717 A. D., London lodges had two and only two reasons in constituting a Grand Lodge: the first was to establish a center of union and harmony, the other was to revive the Annual Feasts.[1]

A dinner is nothing but a meal; a Feast, however, is neither a dinner nor a banquet, it is an occasion. On these special nights a lodge would be created by setting up tables in the form of a semi-circle, and an altar in the middle with the Holy Bible, square and compasses accompanied by three burning tapers. A Table Lodge is part of the mysteries of the order and should be conducted as such. Therefore, a Table Lodge should be held in a secure place tiled as a lodge room. There is one major difference between a Table Lodge and a Festive Board that usually causes a misconception.

A Table Lodge is a Lodge meeting, therefore it should be tiled. Traditionally the Table Lodge was where lodge business stated meetings were held. So just as Masonic meetings are tiled today, Table Lodges should also be tiled. A Festive Board is simply what it states, a festive meeting, a social event, so tiling such a meeting is not required. The main difference is that a Table Lodge is open only to Masons. However, in both a Festive Board and Table Lodge members raise their glasses and share in Masonic Toasts and songs. [2]

97

The hall in which the Table Lodge is held should be so situated that no one without can see or overhear anything within. The table is set up as neatly as possible and in the shape of a horseshoe. The table should be large enough, if the location allows, permitting all to be seated in the outer side of the table. The semi-circle represented half a revolution, or a period of 6 months. Each semicircle is emblematical of the time that passes between each Table Lodge, or more appropriately each Feast of St. John. The brethren would all be properly clothed according to their Masonic degrees, and a Tiler posted to guard against the approach of cowans and eavesdroppers. The Worshipful Master sat at the head of the table or the base of the U, which should be situated in the east. The Wardens are seated at either column or legs of the U, at the ends of the table. The Senior Warden is seated at the end of the table on the right of the Worshipful Master, or the north column. The Junior Deacon is seated on the immediate left of the

Senior Warden. The Junior Warden is seated on the end of the table on the left of the Worshipful Master, or the south column. The Senior Steward is seated on the immediate right of the Junior Warden, and the Junior Steward on his immediate left. On the direct right of the Worshipful Master sat a distinguished guest, or guest of honor, on his right the Chaplain, on his right the Treasurer. At the end of the base of the U sat the Senior Deacon, basically the north east corner. On the immediate left of the Worshipful Master sat the Secretary; the remaining brethren did not have assigned seats. However, if any Entered Apprentices or Fellowcrafts are present, they should be seated in the North, or the Senior Warden's Column under the direction of the Senior Deacon. All that constitutes the table service should be set in three parallel lines, that is to say, the plates form the first line, the bottles and glasses the second, and the food and lights the third. There should also be a blue firing line running down the middle of the entire U-shaped table marked with chalk, marker, or ribbon. The firing line

is essential, this is where all of the "cannons" are placed

before a toast, so that the Worshipful Master and Wardens

may see that all cannons are properly charged and aligned.

As in all Masonic undertakings, the Table lodge is formally

opened with an invocation to the Grand Architect as well as

a ritualistic opening. [3]

After the opening rituals the brethren would

participate in the most commonly known part of a Table

Lodge: the Feast, or Festive Board. The Festive Board is a

partaking of bread and wine, known to us in the 21st

century as a dinner feast. During the Table Lodge seven

toasts have to be given, called Santes d'obligation or

Obligatory Toasts. The Obligatory Toasts are to be

dedicated as follows: The first toast is to the Head of State

of a geographical area in which the lodge is operating,

whether it be the President, Queen, etc. The second toast is

given to the head of the organization, such as the Grand

Master, Grand Commander, etc. The third toast is given to the head of that constituent body holding the Table Lodge, such as the Worshipful Master of the Lodge, or the Commander of a Commandery. The fourth toast is given to the Wardens or other presiding officers of the constituent Lodge. The fifth toast is typically given to the armed forces. The sixth toast is given to the other officers of the constituent lodge and any visitors present. Finally the seventh and last toast is known as the Tyler's Toast, given by the Tyler of the Lodge to all Masons wherever they may be. These seven libations were made in ancient banquets in honor of the seven ancient planets. The Sun, Moon, Mars, Mercury, Jupiter, Venus, and Saturn, they are also made to commemorate the seven days of the week, which are named after them. The Sun for Sunday, Moon for Monday, Mars for Tuesday, Mercury for Wednesday, Jupiter for Thursday, Venus for Friday, and Saturn for Saturday. Sunday is easily understood in English why it is named after the Sun, Monday for the Moon, and Saturday after Saturn, but for the remaining days one has to look for the origin or Latin naming of the days of the week. Dies Martis means Tuesday, dies Mercurii means Wednesday, dies Jovis means Thursday, and dies Veneris means Friday. The astrological account for the seven days of the week can be better explained alchemically.[4]

Once a Table Lodge is opened, everyone in attendance is obligated to use the Table Lodge vocabulary. For example, napkins are called flags, lights are stars, knives are swords and glasses are cannons. The reason for this is to keep with the ancient traditions, and to represent ancient and modern Freemasonry according to the 18th century rituals. Typically, the 18th century Table Lodge rituals derived from military fashioned proceedings. Therefore all of the objects in the room took a military name, usually of naval background. The full Table Lodge Vocabulary is a follows.

Table cloth – Standard, Napkin – Flags, Table –
Tracing Boards, Dishes – Great Plates, Plates –
Tiles, Spoons – Trowels, Knives – Swords, Forks –
Pickaxes, Bottles – Casks, Glasses – Cannons,
Lights – Stars, Chairs – Stalls, Meals – Materials,
Bread – Rough Ashlars, Red Wine – Strong Red
Powder, White Wine – Strong White Powder,
Water – Weak Powder, Beer – Yellow Powder,
Coffee – Black Powder, Brandy – Fulminating
Powder, Salt – White sand, Pepper – Cement, To
Eat – To Masticate, To Drink – Fire, To Carve – To
Hew.[5]

The drinking is done by rule and led by the

Worshipful Master, and everyone in attendance must

participate. The cannons would be charged with strong or

weak powder, meaning everyone's glasses or cannons are

filled with either wine (strong powder) or juice (weak

powder). The Worshipful Master will then ask the Wardens

if the cannons are charged in their columns. Once they are

charged, the Worshipful Master raps everyone up and the

toast is given. After each toast is given the Worshipful

Master says, "aim", at which point everyone raises his glass

and waits for the order of the Master to Fire. Once the

Master orders the "fire" the drinking is done in three motions: first by bringing the glass to lips; then drinking; and finally slamming the glass on the table. The noise the slamming makes is supposed to represent the firing of canons, hence glasses being called cannons. The Good Fire will be called and led by the proposer of the toast immediately following the toast, and before the Brethren are seated. In ancient times, especially in the French Rite, the Good Fire was given using heavy-bottomed "firing glasses" or "cannons" which were struck upon the table in unison with the proposer's cadence. First on the far side the plate, then on the left and then on the right, in order to show the brethren seated across and on either side that you had properly drained your glass. In more modern times, the English developed the practice of delivering the Good Fire with the glass not in hand by simply pointing with the right index finger. The battery of salutes consist of seven triads, 21 motions in all. The good fire represents a 21-gun salute, which is traditionally given only to heads of state, and was originally given by rapping the firing glasses on the table 21 times. The breakage of glasses inspired the more harmless forms of the good fire used today, by leaving the glasses on the table after the toast. The proposer will call a good fire and recite at a smart pace, marking time with his right index finger in the air; all present follow the cadence set by the proposer. "Point, left, right. Point left right. Point left right. One, two, clap. Clap, clap, clap. Clap, clap, clap. Clap, clap, clap." Theoretically, each set of "Point Left Right" is supposed to form a Trinity in the shape of an equilateral triangle. Each equilateral triangle is supposed to represent the due-guard of each Masonic degree. [6]

In the eighteenth century lodges, the feast bulked so large in the life of the lodge that in many of them the members were seated at the table when the lodges were opened and remained at it throughout the Communication, even when degrees were conferred.[7]

Today, Table Lodges are practiced all over the world, predominantly observed in Europe. Sadly, in the United States this very ancient and celebrated tradition is slowly becoming a forgotten Masonic practice, although, a number of Lodges, Chapters, Councils and Commanderies still try to keep the tradition alive. In some Grand Lodges such as the Grand Lodge of Alabama, Table Lodges are avoided like the plague. While in others such as Maine or Wisconsin, they are observed with some previsions and watched over by the Grand Lodge. In the Grand Lodge of Texas, there are several lodges, which take part in either a Festive Board or Table Lodge. Tranquility Lodge No. 2000 holds a Festive Board after meetings, Jacques DeMolay No. 1390 and Holland Lodge No. 1 in Houston usually hold an annual Table Lodge, often in April. Every November, St Alban's Lodge No 1455 in College Station, holds a more

Traditional and renowned Table Lodge. Every March, Anson Jones Knight Masons Council No. 47 holds a Table Lodge or Table Council since they are a Council, to commemorate St. Patrick. The second Saturday in February, during Masonic Week in Washington D.C., Adoniram Council No 43 A. M. D. holds their famous annual Table Council. Independent Royal Arch Lodge No. 2 in New York City, New York, and Lessing Passaic Lodge No 67 in Passaic, New Jersey, are known for having probably the best Table Lodges in the country. Finally, there is Gray Lodge No. 329 in Houston, Texas, which holds two very traditional Table Lodges every year, one after the December stated meeting to commemorate St. John the Evangelist, and the other after the election of officers in June to commemorate St. John the Baptist.* Traditional Table Lodges should be held twice a year, once in December and once in June. This tradition was established to commemorate the two St.'s John, St. John the

Baptist and St. John the Evangelist, the two eminent patron Saints of Freemasonry; 27 December is St John the Evangelist's day, and 24 June is St. John the Baptist's day. Since the Grand Lodge of Texas does not have an adopted ritual for Table Lodge proceedings, I attended numerous Table Lodges and did extensive research on the subject. After many long hours of writing and compiling, the ritual Gray Lodge uses today was created and on 5 December, 2007 the first Gray Lodge Table Lodge was held, presided over by W.M. Lex Leckie.

As American Lodges became larger, and as the various Grand Lodges came into being, the Table Lodge disappeared for many years because of objections to the use of alcoholic beverages for the toasts that were drunk throughout the ceremony. In recent years, the Table Lodge has been revived in a few Grand Jurisdictions in the United States, but most of those lodges use a fruit juice or other non-alcoholic beverage for the toast. In some jurisdictions the program has to be approved by the Grand Lodge, in others a dispensation must be granted, in some a Grand Lodge Officer must be present, while in others the Grand Lodge has a prescribed Table Lodge Ritual, and in very few cases the use of wine is optional. It is also interesting to note that in some Grand Jurisdictions in the United States, the Table Lodge Rituals differ on the number of the "traditional" toasts. In some it may be five, in some seven, while others might have as many as eleven. In the United States John M. Hilliard, Past Master of Independent Royal Arch No 2 in New York should be credited as being the pioneer in Masonic Table Lodges. In England however, the brethren usually gather at the Festive Board following their meetings. No matter how it is portrayed, a Table Lodge should be an extravaganza of Masonic fellowship, of feasts, lectures and togetherness. The brethren should be gathered in the spirit of traditional Masonry, traditional being that of the origin of speculative masonry.

Appendix A

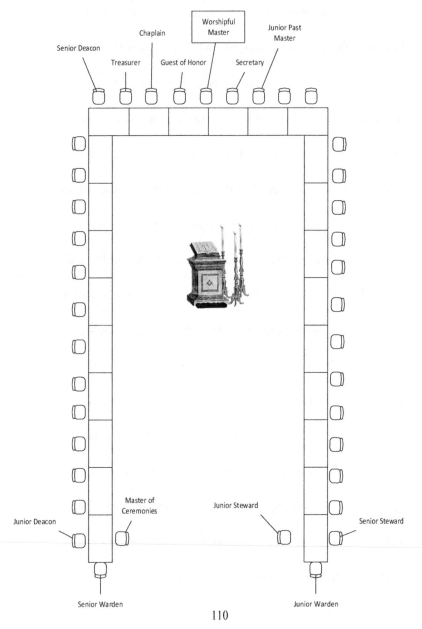

Appendix B

The following is the Gray Lodge No. 329 A.F &

A.M. Table Lodge ritual in its entirety:

W.M. (Worshipful Master raps up Lodge)

W.M. Brethren, let us pray.

Chaplain: Supreme Grand Master of the Universe, we would reverently invoke Thy blessing at this time. Wilt Thou be pleased to grant that this meeting, thus begun in order, may be conducted in peace and closed in harmony. Amen.

All: So mote it be.

(**W.M.** seats Lodge, and then raps twice. Wardens rise.)

W.M. Brothers Senior and Junior Warden, invite our Brethren in the columns of the West and South to assist us in opening a Table Lodge in the Entered Apprentice degree.

S.W. Brethren in the West, assist us in opening a Table Lodge in the Entered Apprentice degree.

J.W. Brethren in the South, assist us in opening a Table Lodge in the Entered Apprentice degree.

W.M. Brethren, assist us in opening a Table Lodge of Instruction. (Pauses) Brother Senior Warden, are you a Mason?

S.W. All my Brethren know me as such.

W.M. What is the first care of a Mason?

S.W. To see that the Lodge is Tyled.

W.M. Satisfy yourself that such is the case.

S.W. Bro. J.D., you will ascertain if this Lodge is Tyled. (J.D. goes to Tyled door, reports to Tyler, Tyles the door, returns to place, reports to S.W. "It is.")

S.W. It is, Worshipful.

W.M. What is the second care of a Mason?

S.W. To see if the Brethren are in order.

W.M. Are they in order?

S.W. (Assures that all are properly vouched for in the usual manner) they are in order Worshipful.

W.M. Why are we met together?

S.W. To erect Temples to virtue and dig dungeons for vices, and to hold an extravaganza of Masonic Fellowship, composed of feasts, lectures and togetherness.

W.M. How long must we work?

S.W. From High Twelve to Low Twelve

W.M. What is the hour?

S. W. High Twelve.

W.M. In consideration of the hour, inform our Brethren that an Entered Apprentice Masons Lodge is now open for the purpose of a Table lodge of Instruction, and that we are about to begin our work in the usual manner.

S.W. (Raps up Lodge) Brethren in the West, in consideration of the hour, the Worshipful Master has ordered an Entered Apprentice Masons Lodge to be opened for the purpose of a Table Lodge of Instruction, and we are about to begin our work in the usual manner.

J.W. Brethren in the South, you have heard the Senior Warden. Let it so be done.

W.M. Together brethren Du-Gu (E.A.)

W.M. One rap
S.W. One rap
J.W. One rap

W. M.: In the name of God and the holy Saints John, I now declare this Table Lodge duly open.

W.M. (Master seats Lodge.) One rap

Food is served

after all are seated

113

FIRST TOAST

W.M. One rap
S.W. One rap
J.W. One rap

W.M. Brothers Senior and Junior Wardens, cause the arms to be charged and aligned for the first toast of obligation .

S.W. Brethren on my column, in all your grades and stations, charge and align your arms for the first toast of obligation which the Worshipful Master is about to propose.

J.W. Brethren on my column, in all your grades and stations, charge and align your arms for the first toast of obligation which the Worshipful Master is about to propose.

W.M. Brothers Senior and Junior Wardens, are the cannons charged and aligned?

S.W. Yes, Worshipful.

J. W. Yes, Worshipful.

W.M. (Three raps - all rise) Brothers Senior and Junior Wardens, announce to our Brethren that the toast which I have the pleasure to propose is that to the President of the United States.

S.W. Brethren on my column, in all our grades and stations, the toast which the Worshipful Master has the pleasure to propose is that to the President of the United States.

J.W. Brethren on my column, in all our grades and stations, the toast which the Worshipful Master has the pleasure to propose is that to the President of the United States.

W.M. Brethren, to the President of the United States.

ALL: To the President of the United States.

W.M. Aim: (The glass is raised.)

W.M.: Fire; (drinking done in three motions)

W.M. one rap

SECOND TOAST

W.M. (while seated) One rap

S.W. One rap

J.W. One rap

W.M. Brothers Senior and Junior Wardens, cause the arms to be charged and aligned for the second toast of obligation.

S.W. Brethren on my column in all your grades and stations, charge and align your arms for the second toast of obligation which the Worshipful Master is about to propose.

J.W. Brethren on my column in all your grades and stations, charge and align your arms for the second toast of obligation which the Worshipful Master is about to propose.

W.M. Brothers Senior and Junior Wardens, are the cannons charged and aligned?

S.W. Yes, Worshipful.

J.W. Yes, Worshipful.

W.M. (Three raps). (all rise.)

W.M. Brothers Senior and Junior Wardens, announce to our Brethren that the toast which I have the pleasure to propose is that to the Most Worshipful Grand Master and the Most Worshipful Grand Lodge of Texas.

S.W. Brethren on my column in all your grades and stations, the toast which the Worshipful Master has the pleasure to propose is that to the Most Worshipful Grand Master and the Most Worshipful Grand Lodge of Texas.

J.W. Brethren on my column in all your grades and stations, the toast which the Worshipful Master has the pleasure to propose is that to the Most Worshipful Grand Master and the Most Worshipful Grand Lodge of Texas.

W.M. Brethren, to the Most Worshipful Grand Master and the Most Worshipful Grand Lodge of Texas.

ALL To the Most Worshipful Grand Master and the Most Worshipful Grand Lodge of Texas.

W.M. Aim: (The glass is raised.)

W.M. Fire: (drinking done in three motions)

W.M. one rap

THIRD TOAST
S.W. One rap
J.W. One rap
W.M. One rap

W.M. Brothers Senior and Junior Wardens, what do you desire?

S.W. Worshipful Master, the brother Junior Warden and I beg to allow the arms to be charged and aligned for a toast that we wish to propose.

W.M. Brethren in all your grades and stations, charge and align your arms for a toast that our brothers the wardens wish to propose.

W.M Brothers Senior and Junior Warden, are all the cannons charged and aligned?

S.W. Yes, Worshipful.

J.W. Yes, Worshipful.

W. M. (Three raps) (all rise) The East yields to your desire. What is the toast that a wish to propose?

S.W. It is to you, Worshipful. Brethren on my column in all your grades and stations, the toast which the Junior Warden and I have the pleasure to propose is that to our Worshipful Master.

J.W. Brethren on my column in all your grades and stations, the toast which the Senior Warden and I have the pleasure to propose is that to our Worshipful Master.

S.W. Brethren, to our Worshipful Master:

ALL To our Worshipful Master.

W.M. Aim: (The glass is raised.)

W.M. Fire: (drinking done in three motions)

W.M. one rap

FOURTH TOAST

W.M. One rap
S.W. One rap
J.W. One rap

W.M. Brothers Senior and Junior Wardens, cause the arms to be charged and aligned for the fourth toast of obligation.

S.W. Brethren on my column in all your grades and stations, charge and align your arms for the fourth toast of obligation which the Worshipful Master is about to propose.

J.W. Brethren on my column in all your grades and stations, charge and align your arms for the fourth toast of obligation which the Worshipful Master is about to propose.

W.M. Brothers Senior and Junior Wardens, are all the cannons charged and aligned?

S.W. Yes, Worshipful.

J.W. Yes, Worshipful.

W.M. (Three raps) (All rise) Brothers Senior and Junior Wardens, announce to our Brethren that the toast which I have the pleasure to propose is that to the Wardens.

S.W. Brethren on my column in all your grades and stations, the toast which the Worshipful Master has the pleasure to propose is that to the Wardens.

J.W. Brethren on my column in all your grades and stations, the toast which the Worshipful Master has the pleasure to propose is that to the Wardens.

W.M. Brethren, to the Wardens:

ALL To the Wardens.

W.M. Aim: (The glass is raised.)

W.M. Fire: (drinking done in three motions)

W.M. One rap

Fifth TOAST

W.M. One rap
S.W. One rap
J.W. One rap

W.M. Brothers Senior and Junior Wardens, cause the arms to be charged and aligned for the fifth toast of obligation.

S.W. Brethren on my column in all your grades and stations, charge and align your arms for the fifth toast of obligation which the Worshipful Master is about to propose.

J.W. Brethren on my column in all your grades and stations, charge and align your arms for the fifth toast of obligation which the Worshipful Master is about to propose.

W.M. Brothers Senior and Junior Wardens are all the cannons charged and aligned?

S.W. Yes, Worshipful.

J.W. Yes, Worshipful.

W.M. (Three raps) (All rise) Brothers Senior and Junior Wardens, announce to our Brethren that the toast which I have the pleasure to propose is that to the Brethren in the Armed Forces..

S.W. Brethren on my column in all your grades and stations, the toast which the Worshipful Master has the pleasure to propose is that to the Brethren in the Armed Forces.

J.W. Brethren on my column in all your grades and stations, the toast which the Worshipful Master has the pleasure to propose is that to the Brethren in the Armed Forces

W.M. Brethren, to the Brethren in the Armed Forces:

ALL To the Brethren in the Armed Forces.

W.M. Aim: (The glass is raised.)

W.M. Fire: (drinking done in three motions)

W.M. One rap

Sixth Toast

W.M.   One rap
S.W.   One rap
J.W.   One rap

W.M. Brothers Senior and Junior Wardens, cause the arms to be charged and aligned for the sixth toast of obligation.

S.W. Brethren on my column in all your grades and stations, charge and align your arms for the sixth toast of obligation which the Worshipful Master is about to propose.

J.W. Brethren on my column in all your grades and stations, charge and align your arms for the sixth toast of obligation which the Worshipful Master is about to propose.

W.M. Brothers Senior and Junior Wardens, are all the cannons charged and aligned?

S.W. Yes, Worshipful.

J.W. Yes, Worshipful.

W.M. (Three raps) (All rise) Brothers Senior and Junior Wardens, announce to our Brethren that the toast which I have the pleasure to propose is that to the other officers and visiting Brethren.

S.W. Brethren on my column in all your grades and stations, the toast which the Worshipful Master has the pleasure to propose is that to the other officers and visiting Brethren.

J.W. Brethren on my column all your grades and stations, the toast which the Worshipful Master has the pleasure to propose is that to the other officers and visiting Brethren.

W.M. Brethren, to the other officers and visiting Brethren:

ALL To the other officers and visiting Brethren.

W.M. Aim: (The glass is raised.)

W.M. Fire: (drinking done in three motions)

W.M. One rap

Seventh TOAST

W.M. One rap
S.W. One rap
J.W. One rap

W.M. Brothers Senior and Junior Wardens, cause the arms to be charged and aligned for the seventh toast of obligation.

S.W. Brethren on my column in all your grades and stations, charge and align your arms for the seventh toast of obligation which the Worshipful Master is about to propose.

J.W. Brethren on my column in all your grades and stations, charge and align your arms for the seventh toast of obligation which the Worshipful Master is about to propose.

W.M. Brothers Senior and Junior Wardens, are all the cannons charged and aligned?

S.W. Yes, Worshipful.

J.W. Yes, Worshipful.

123

W.M. (Three raps) (all rise) Brothers Senior and Junior Wardens, announce to our Brethren that the toast which I have the pleasure to propose is that to all Masons where so ever dispersed over the face of the globe.

S.W. Brethren on my column all your grades and stations, the toast which the Worshipful Master has the pleasure to propose is that to all Masons where so ever dispersed over the face of the globe.

J.W. Brethren on my column all your grades and stations, the toast which the Worshipful Master has the pleasure to propose is that to all Masons where so ever dispersed over the face of the globe.

W.M. Brethren, to all Masons where so ever dispersed over the face of the globe.

ALL To all Masons where so ever dispersed over the face of the globe.

W.M. Aim: (The glass is raised.)

W.M.: Fire: (drinking done in three motions)

W.M. One rap

CLOSE

W.M. Brothers Senior and Junior Wardens, are all the Brethren in order?

S.W. They are, Worshipful.
J.W. They are, Worshipful.

W.M. What is the hour?
S.W. Low twelve.

W.M. In consideration of the hour, inform all our Brethren both on the west and south that we are about to close this Table Lodge ending our work in the usual manner.

S.W. Brethren on my column, I inform you on behalf of the Worshipful Master that we are about to close this Table Lodge ending our work in the usual manner.

J.W. Brethren on my column, I inform you on behalf of the Worshipful Master that we are about to close this Table Lodge, ending our work in the usual manner.

W.M. (Worshipful master raps up Lodge)

W. M.: Together brethren Du-Gu (E.A.)

W.M. Brethren, let us pray.

Chaplin Brethren – Before the Lodge is closed, let us, with all reverence and humility, express our gratitude to the Great Architect of the Universe, for the blessings already received. May he continue to preserve the order, by cementing and adorning it with every social and moral virtue. Amen.

All: So mote it be.

W.M. One rap
S.W. One rap
J.W. One rap

W. M. In the name of God and the holy Saints John I now declare this Table Lodge duly closed. [8]

Appendix C

NOTES

[1]   "Table Lodge," Coil's Masonic Encyclopedia (Richmond, Virginia: Macoy, 1995), 388; "History   of the Table Lodge," *Transactions of the Texas Lodge of Research, A.F. & A. M.* 13 (1978): 178-   179.

[2]   "Masonic Feast, Banquets and Table Lodges" (The Masonic Service Association., Maryland,   1986)1-4, 14-28.

[3]   Table Lodge, Coil, 388; Masonic Feast, Masonic Service Association, 1-28; "Table Lodge,   "Albert G. Mackey, *An Encyclopedia of Freemasonry,* ed., rev. and enl. By Robert L. Clegg, 2 vols (Chicago: Masonic History, 1929), 2 1008.

[4]   Rex R. Hutchens, *A Bridge to Light* (Washington, D.C.: The Supreme Council, 2006) 224-250; "History of the Table Lodge," *Transactions of the Texas Lodge of Research, A.F. & A. M.* 13 (1978): 178-179; Table Lodge, Mackey, 1008; "Toast, "Albert G. Mackey, *An Encyclopedia of Freemasonry,* ed., rev. and enl. By Robert L. Clegg, 2 vols (Chicago: Masonic History, 1929), 2 1041-1042.

[5]   Table Lodge, Mackey, 1008.; Toast, Mackey, 1041-1042.

[6]   Table Lodge, Coil, 388; "Table Lodge, Mackey, 1008; "Toast, Mackey, 1041-   1042.; "Masonic Feast, Banquets and Table Lodges" (The Masonic Service Association., Maryland, 1986)1-4, 14- 28; Joseph Crociata, "The Table Lodge: A Celebration of Universal Fellowship," *The Voice of Freemasonry* 2 (Vol 22): 16-19; "Table Council" (The Adoniram Council No. 43 Allied Masonic Degrees., New York City, 2008),2-6.

[7]   Masonic Feast, Masonic Service Association, 1-28.

[8]   Roberto M. Sanchez, *Gray Lodge No. 329 Table Lodge Ritual* (Gray Lodge 329,2007), 1-11.

*Written prior to the moratorium on Table Lodges by the Grand Lodge of Texas

Chapter Four

THE CHAMBER OF REFLECTION: A REVITALIZED AND MISUNDERSTOOD MASONIC PRACTICE

Though the initiation rituals of Freemasonry are universal with slight variation according to various Grand Lodge jurisdiction, most American lodges fail to incorporate one of the oldest traditions utilized to prepare candidates through the use of the chamber of reflection. Prior to 2009, the majority of Masons in the United States were unaware of the use of the chamber of reflection as an accepted preparation practice for the degrees. The chamber of reflection was not a phrase common to pop culture, or even a part of American Freemasonry. However, thanks to author Dan Brown and his best-selling thriller *The Lost Symbol*, it has become a growing trend in many American Masonic lodges. Those Freemasons who are members of the York Rite, more especially the Commandery, are tacitly familiar with the chamber of reflection. Yet, even these degrees provide scant explanation in any of the rituals. Somewhere in the transition towards a modern American society, the true intent of the chamber of reflection vanished into the mist of antiquity. It is the purpose of this author to explore the history, protocol, and traditions of the chamber of reflection. While traveling to several Grand jurisdictions in several different countries, I discovered that the chamber of reflection is very much alive where it has been continually practiced for years. Most of the brethren who received their initiations in Europe, Mexico, Central and South America, the Middle East and Africa will be acquainted with the chamber of reflection. Lastly, the practice may be found in the degrees in the Ancient and

Accepted Scottish Rite, the French Rite, the Brazilian Rite and other rites derived from those listed.

In *The Lost Symbol,* a fictional thriller involving the Freemasons, Dan Brown introduces to the reader one of Freemasonry's greatest initiatory tools - the chamber of reflection.

"The skull sat atop a rickety wooden desk positioned against the rear wall of the chamber. Two human leg bones sat beside the skull, along with a collection of other items that were meticulously arranged on the desk in shrine like fashion - an antique hourglass, a crystal flask, a candle, two saucers of pale powder, and a sheet of paper. Propped against the wall beside the desk stood the fearsome shape of a long scythe, its curved blade as familiar as that of the grim reaper... 'This room is Masonic?' Sato demanded, turning from the skull and staring at Langdon in the darkness. Langdon nodded calmly, 'it's called a Chamber of Reflection. These rooms are designed as cold, austere places in which a Mason can reflect on his own mortality. By meditating on the inevitability of death, a Mason gains valuable perspective on the fleeting nature of life.' "

Dan Brown goes on to paint a vivid picture of the meaning of the chamber of reflection and lists items found in such a place. But what did all of this mean to the Freemasons?

How many American Freemason could actually identify the meaning of the items in this "secret room"?[1]

The chamber of reflection is not a new innovation but an ancient tradition older than the Craft itself. In Freemasonry, the chamber of reflection was originally found in the French and Scottish Rites. This small room, usually adjacent to the lodge, is the predecessor of what Freemasons, commonly call the "anteroom." The purpose of the chamber of reflection is to give the candidate a chance to prepare himself for his initiation into the Fraternity. It is not just for the external preparation of the candidate, to put on the required garments, but for the internal mental preparation of the candidate. The candidate is encouraged through self reflection to contemplate what his motives are for joining the lodge. The chamber of reflection is exactly what it implies, a quiet room where the candidate is to meditate before his initiation. Isolation in this cavern-like room is where a symbolic metamorphosis is experienced, the neophyte emerges from this chamber symbolically transformed into a new person. It serves to separate the candidate of all earthly things, his family, his job, the superfluities of daily life, and makes him consider the notions of his own mortality. The chamber of reflection was intended to be the candidate's very first experience in Masonry. However, it is important to note that the chamber of reflection is a preparation tool, and not part of the degree itself. [2]

There are slight variations to the contents located within a chamber of reflection. For the context of this paper, the most common items as listed in the rituals of the French and Scottish Rite will be referenced. According to Albert Pike, the chamber of reflection "should be one story below the lodge room; and if possible, underground, with no window. The floor must, in any case, be of earth. On the walls should be brief sentences of morality, and maxims austere philosophy, written as if with charcoal." The room should be completely dark, and the walls painted black or made to look like the interior of a cave. In the center of the room is placed a small wooden table, accompanied by a stool or uncomfortable wooden chair for the candidate to sit on. On the table the following items should be somberly placed: a single lit candle, a human skull and crossed tibia (leg bones), an hour glass, a small bell, a small loaf of bread, a basin of water, containers of salt, sulphur, and mercury, a mirror, papers, a quill pen and ink. In some chambers of reflection, there may be a picture or representation of a rooster instead of the mercury. Lastly the alchemical cipher V∴I∴T∴R∴ I∴O∴L∴, and the words "Know Thyself" should be written somewhere on the wall.[3]

The emblems and relics found in a chamber of reflection all have a very specific significance. Before expanding on these symbols, let us follow a candidate's journey into the chamber of reflection on the day of his initiation into this tradition. First the candidate, dressed in suitable lodge attire (dark suit and tie) is brought to the lodge building by his sponsor. He must not meet any of the other Mason except the ones necessary. The Secretary and the Master of Ceremonies, (an officer who in some jurisdictions would be equivalent to the First Expert,) both dressed without any Masonic insignia, meet the candidate. The Secretary collects the necessary fees and returns to the lodge room. The Master of Ceremonies stays with the candidate, while the sponsor also goes into the lodge room. The Master of Ceremonies then blindfolds the candidate and introduces him into the chamber of reflection. He presents the candidate with a piece of paper with questions that the candidate must answer. The Master of Ceremonies indicates to the candidate that he must write on the paper his moral and philosophical testament. He then instructs the candidate that when he has finished this task, he should ring the bell, or give three knocks to acknowledge that he is ready to proceed with the rest of the initiation. He is also told that, once the door is closed, he should remove the hoodwink. At that time, the candidate sees the chamber and the objects described earlier.[4]

The chamber of reflection is an important symbol. It represents a womblike state, where the aspirant is to participate in his rebirth as an initiate, to indicate when the candidate emerges from the chamber, in the same manner as being born a new man. Thus, the chamber indicates at the same time, a beginning and an end. The end of the candidate's life as a profane, and the beginning of a new life as an initiate in search of more light. According to Andrew Hammer, in his book *Observing the Craft,*

"Before ever knocking at the door of the Craft, the initiate was confronted with the gravity of his choice to join, so that any doubts he might have entertained could be acted upon. In this way he might be spared a commitment he has not truly resolved to make, and the Lodge spared a man who would not endure even the test of confronting himself, much less having the resolve to better that which he had confronted. He is put in darkness and isolation because both of these things together decrease the perception of time, and make a relatively short period of time seem much longer. Thus, when the initiate arrives at the door of a Lodge, he has, to mind, long been in darkness."

This is the beginning of the journey for each candidate as they embark into the mystical and dramatic realm of Freemasonry. It is at this point the candidate stands at the threshold of initiation where he may turn back. Yet, if he chooses to proceed his life will be forever transformed. If the candidate fails to progress through the work of the remaining degrees, by their experiences in the outer chamber will force them to reflect upon their reason for wishing to become a Mason, and as such, for all their actions in life.[5]

The most misunderstood emblem is the skull. For centuries many non-masons and some persons within the Fraternity believed the skull to be an immoral and malicious symbol. It represented a malevolent and evil nature, such as poison or danger. But in the chamber of reflection, as in the rest of Masonry, that is not the case.

The skull has appeared for centuries in various Masonic degrees, tracing boards, and aprons, such as the nineteenth century Knight Templar apron. The skull, together with the crossbones, is a symbol of mortality, and is used to elaborate on the other symbols present in the chamber. Its' purpose is to serve as a reminder of the Latin phrase *memento mori*, "remember, you will die." It serves as a reminder that our earthly life is not eternal and your time spent on this earth is limited and should be spent to improve society, yourself, and your spiritual service. Death is eminent, and each of us at one point or another must face this ultimate ending.[6]

The hourglass is an emblem of human life and represents the passing or marking of time. It symbolizes the futility of attempting to stop or to slow down time. As the candidate watches the slowly falling sands running through the hourglass so too does his time slowly runs out to death. The hourglass elaborates on the solemn thought of death, and reminds the candidate of the fleeting nature of his mortality. Together the skull, the hourglass alludes to mortality and reminds the future Mason to make good use of his short time on Earth.[7]

The bread and water represent the bare necessities of life and are humble emblems of sustenance and simplicity. Bread, considered one of the most meager forms of nourishment, reminds the candidate to live his life plainly, simply and humbly. Water is one of the four elements essential to the ancient mysteries, and is also an emblem of purity, or cleansing. In some variations of the chamber of reflection, the candidate is required to wash his hands as a symbol of the purity of his intentions.[8]

The burning candle and bell lack some of the esoteric significance attached to the other emblems but are also important. The bell is rarely used since it takes up space on the small table used in the chamber of reflection. It's sole purpose is to inform the Master of Ceremonies, or the Mason in charge of the candidate while he is in the chamber, that the candidate is ready for the degree. Most common the candidate knocking three times on the door, has replaced the bell at the completion of his mental preparation. The single burning candle primarily serves to provide the candidate with suitable lighting so he may perform the assigned task, whether it be writing his philosophical last will and testament, required questions or thoughts, all depending on the Masonic jurisdiction, or practiced Masonic rite. [9]

There are several items associated with alchemy in the chamber of reflection. To begin the ultimate goal of an alchemist was to turn a crude and superfluous metal into a prosperous and valuable metal such as transforming lead into gold. In the chamber of reflection, the alchemical elements are there to represent a different transformation, that of transforming the petitioner into a candidate. These alchemical elements are salt, sulfur and mercury. Salt alludes to several uses, but in the alchemical sense it alludes to the human soul. Salt is a preservative, and reminds the candidate that his activities while on earth should be remembered in a positive manner even after death. Salt, in excess may also spoil the food it was intended to preserve and admonishes the candidate to moderate his desires and passions. [10]

Sulfur refers to the human body since some forms of sulfur are found in hair and skin. It is also a mindful reminder that all trials come to pass. Just as the foul odor of the sulfur will dissipate over time, so shall any trials and tribulations the candidate may encounter. It serves as a lesson, and reminds the candidate to make all things a learning experience. The coupling of salt and sulphur are the equivalent of the checkered pavement. It represents that of ambivalence and balance of light and darkness, truth and error, life and death, soul and body. [11]

Mercury may appear in the chamber of reflection as the element itself, or it may be symbolically represented as a rooster or cockerel, either painted or as a ceramic figurine. The rooster is a symbol for the Greek god Hermes, or the Roman god Mercury, who crows at the dawn of day announcing the coming of light. This alludes to vigilance and also corresponds with faith. Mercury is a symbol of the emergence of the darkness of ignorance and fear. It is also the omen foretelling spiritual trial and testing. Just as we need vigilance and perseverance to seek truth and the light, we must also have the courage to acknowledge it when our social standing, ego, and perception from others challenge it. Mercury, salt, and sulfur, together, allude to the makeup of man and all substances. These three symbolic elements derive from alchemy, a tradition which has provided us with all of the symbols we use today to describe a metamorphosis, thereby alluding to a lesson the candidate will learn in the first degree—to circumscribe his desires and keep his passions in due bounds. [12]

The quill pen and paper are placed in the chamber of reflection for the candidate to perform his appointed task of writing as he is instructed. Depending upon the particular Rite or degree, the candidate is asked to compose a short piece of writing. Most common, however, the candidate is encouraged to write reasons for petitioning for the degrees, or, in some lodges, his moral and philosophical last will and testament. Since the candidate is confronted with the thoughts of his own mortality, he is asked to put into writing where all of his worldly belongings and legacy would go in case of his ultimate demise. In some variations, specifically in the advanced degrees of the York Rite, there is a Bible on the table, and the candidate is asked to read the verse or verses associated with the degree. In the Brazilian Rite, the candidate receives yet another task in addition to the ones already mentioned. He is presented with Articles I and II of the Constitution of the respective Jurisdiction. The candidate must then sign and declare to affirm solidarity and act accordingly to the principles of Freemasonry. In some of the lodges around the world, where the chamber of reflection is used, it is customary to invite the initiate back into the chamber of reflection on his fifth year anniversary of his initiation. He then is presented with the same emblems he saw before his initiation, but now he is also presented with his philosophical and moral last will and testament. The purpose of this exercise is for the initiate to reflect on his initiation, and see how far he has come and transformed over the years. This practice may be repeated on different Masonic anniversaries. In all, this portion of the chamber of reflection allows the candidate a chance to reconsider his request for membership. If his motives are not pure, if he is fearful and does not have the courage to proceed, then he may not be able to inviolate the secrets of Freemasonry. [13]

The alchemical cipher V∴I∴T∴R∴ I∴O∴L∴ is an important element in some versions of the chamber of reflection. It is an acronym for the Latin phrase *Visita Interiora Terrae Rectificando Invenies Occultum Lapidem*, which means, "Visit the interior of the Earth, and by rectifying, you shall find the hidden stone." Sometimes this acronym appears with the addition of U∴M∴ at the end, signifying, V*eram Medicinam*, which means the "true medicine". As previously mentioned, the alchemist's goal was to change base metals into gold, and the acronym *vitriol* was the recipe that would ultimately produce such a transformation. However, in Masonry, the term *vitriol* is used as a tool to remind the candidate to look within himself. Thus, using his time in this solemn chamber to reflect and examine his own life, and therefore search for ways in which he could improve himself internally. Its ultimate goal is to have the candidate reach a sense of self attainment thereby understanding the other saying that should be written in the chamber — Know Thyself. The candidate is to take this advice metaphorically. The meaning conveyed is that one must search within oneself, as the truth is hidden there, and this truth is the real solution to life's problems.[14]

The mirror is essential to the Chamber of Reflection, because the purpose of this portion of the initiation process is to allow the candidate to reflect. He is also to reflect on his own mortality, the reasons he has chosen to join the Craft, and to contemplate his own understanding of himself. According to the lecture in the Third Degree, we are taught that Hiram Abiff repaired to the Holy of Holies to reflect upon the work he had accomplished, to meditate and pray. It is in the chamber of reflection where the candidate gets a chance to practice the teachings of the Craft as they are intended, and emulate our ancient patron. Another example of reflection and looking within oneself is portrayed in the Rectified Scottish

Rite. When the candidate is brought to light in the first degree, and the hoodwink is removed, the first thing he sees are the brethren looking back at him. It is at this point the Worshipful Master informs him that "It is not always before oneself, that one finds his enemies. That which is to be feared the most is many times behind himself. Turn around!" It is at this time that the candidate is once again presented with the mirror and sees his own reflection. It is a lesson by which the candidate is taught that the enemy is usually within oneself. Therefore, each member of the Craft should know and scrutinize himself in order to break off the rough and superfluous parts of his life in order to live the life of a true follower of the Craft. Thus, the chamber of reflection allows the candidate the chance to truly analyze and examine himself and the symbols in the room around him.[15]

The symbols, elements, and lessons within the chamber of reflection are provided for the specific purpose of allowing the candidate to meditate, reflect and contemplate. None of the emblems should ever be used to frighten, haze, tease, or humiliate the candidate in any way. The purpose of the chamber of reflection and its symbolic elements are meant to illustrate to the initiate that the ceremony of initiation is not to be taken lightly.[16]

But what does all of this mean to the American Mason? Where did the Chamber of Reflection go and why is it experiencing a revival in American Freemasonry? The earliest English reference to a Chamber of Reflection seems to be in *Jachin and Boaz,* the English exposure of the ritual of the Ancient's Grand Lodge, published in 1762. Its description strongly resembles that of the one in the French exposure, *Les Secrets de Francs- Maçons,* published in 1742. In *Jachin and Boaz* the chamber of reflection process is explained as follows:

"Soon after, the Master asks if the Gentleman proposed last Lodge-Night is ready to be made; and on being answered in the Affirmative, he orders the Wardens to go out and prepare the Person, who is generally waiting in a Room at some Distance from the Lodge-Room, by himself, being left there by his Friend who proposed him. He is conducted into another Room, which is totally dark; and then asked, whether he is conscious of having the Vocation necessary to be received? On answering, yes, he is asked his Name, Surname, and Profession. When he has answered these Questions, whatever he has about him made of Metal is taken off, as Buckles, Buttons, Rings, Boxes, and even the Money in his pocket taken away. Then they make him uncover his Right Knee, and put his Left Foot with his Shoe on, into a Slipper; hoodwink him with a Handkerchief, and leave him to his Reflection for about half an Hour. The Chamber is also guarded within and without, by some of the Brethren, who have drawn Swords in their Hands, to keep off all Strangers, in case any should dare approach. The Person who proposed the Candidate stays in the Room with him; but they are not permitted to ask any Questions, or converse together."

The idea of the chamber of reflection, as part of Masonic practice, also spread to Germany, Belgium, Holland, and other European countries. Between 1787 and 1801, Friedrich Ludwig Schroeder worked on a revision of the German ritual based on *Jachin and Boaz* entitled *Schroedersches Lehrlingritual*. It was accepted and worked in a number of German lodges, although other versions of the ritual continued to be practiced. [17]

In the early 1800's, the chamber of reflection was being used and practiced in several craft lodges in the United States. By 1814, the chamber of reflection had made its way into the rituals of the Grand Encampment of New York, and by 1816, to General Grand Encampment at its formation. The chamber of reflection was a well understood and a well-practiced Masonic custom in the United States at this epoch of its history. Some Freemasons even had small chambers of reflections in their homes, while others would make it a habit to revisit the one they used during their initiation into the Craft. All of this began to change by 1826, the year that America's most notorious incident involving the Freemasons took place — the Morgan Affair.[18]

Captain William Morgan, a disgruntled Mason, announced plans to publish the rituals of Freemasonry. Although a number of other ritual exposures had been published in the United States during the previous century,

Masons were outraged that their secrets would be divulged to the community. On 11 September 1826, William Morgan was arrested and jailed for an outstanding debt. The next day four Masons paid the debt, bailed Morgan out of jail and escorted him to a waiting carriage. He was driven away and was never seen again. This event fuelled outrage among anti-Masons in the United States and gave birth to the Anti-Masonic political movement. Because of the Anti-Masonic movement, Freemasonry was forced to adapt and change. The laws of several grand jurisdictions were changed, and the old custom of having to be invited or "tapped" to join Masonry were forever changed. Several hundred lodges in the United States closed its doors. New York went from 480 lodges in 1826 to 75 in 1835; Massachusetts dropped from 180 Lodges to 56, and the Grand Lodge of Vermont completely went out of existence. Masonry experienced a transformation of a very exclusive and esoteric fraternity, to that of an open revolving door and transparent fraternity. The more esoteric traditions retreated from the craft lodge into the higher invitational bodies, while the rites and traditions of the craft lodge rituals were diluted or completely abandoned, like that of the chamber of reflection.[19]

According to Masonic researchers and authors S. Brent Morris and Arturo de Hoyos in their book *Committed to the Flames*, in 1826, after the Morgan Affair, Robert Benjamin Folger filled a book with the enciphered craft rituals of a secret Masonic Rite. These rituals were that of the Rectified Scottish Rite, also known as the Knights Beneficent of the Holy City or CBCS. This order was well known throughout Europe but completely unknown in the United States at the time. The chamber of reflection resurrected itself in the United States in rituals such as the Rectified Scottish Rite, but never really returned into mainstream craft lodges until the end of the twentieth century.[20]

Masonry has been forced to adapt and change in order to survive, such as the creation of Masonic fraternal organizations like the Shrine and Grotto, to family oriented ones such as the Order of DeMolay, and Rainbow Girls. Based on the information presented in this paper, chambers of reflection are gaining in popularity again because the younger Masons who are joining lodges today are very interested in the ancient mysteries of the Masonic Orders, and its old traditions. Organizations like the Masonic Restoration Foundation have been created for the purpose of restoring some of these once forgotten Masonic traditions, while at the same time regulating the customs so they will not be done incorrectly. Several grand lodges have adopted a number these customs and traditions in order to regulate them. In a grand masters decision issued 23 January 2013, the Grand Master of Colorado approved the Masonic practices and observances of chambers of reflection, officers processions, and chains of union.[21]

Over the past several years, there have been several articles written about the chamber of reflection with no real research behind them. There are several lodges using chambers of reflection with the goal of scaring the candidate, or doing it because it is a "cool thing to do." If a lodge's members do not know what V∴I∴T∴R∴ I∴O∴L∴ means or represents, and they do not know how to explain it to the new initiate, then that lodge should not be using a chamber of reflection. This important preparatory tool shouldn't be used because it is cool. Rather, it should be used because it helps the candidate prepare himself mentally for the degree, it is an old tradition of the Craft, and it is the correct thing to do. Most importantly, each lodge should practice and follow the constitutions, resolutions, and edicts of the grand lodge under whose jurisdiction it is chartered. In The Laws of The Grand Lodge of Texas, A.F. & A.M., it states that only the ritual approved by the Grand Lodge of Texas may be used in its lodge rooms and ante rooms opening directly into the lodge rooms. However, I find no mention in our grand lodge law regarding or restricting chambers of reflection, or items that may decorate, be stored in, or be present in the preparation room. Furthermore, there are no guidelines as to how the candidate is to be prepared prior to the beginning of the degree.[22]

There is great meaning in the chamber of reflection. A Mason can quietly meditate upon the individual meanings of the contents in the chamber, while reflecting on his purpose for joining, and becoming a better man. More importantly, it removes the candidate from the rest of the membership, who might tease the candidate and advise him to beware of the goat. Throughout my travels in a number of Masonic jurisdictions around the world, I recognized the great importance of this tradition, which has been used for centuries in worldwide Freemasonry. The chamber of reflection should be used prior to each of the three degrees. Every practicing Mason should propose to his respective grand lodge the restoration of the traditional chamber of reflection. This is an important custom that should be restored to every lodge thus allowing the candidate to participate in a *True Masonic Experience*.

Appendix A

The following is a translated Entered Apprentice

Chamber of Reflection Ritual in its entirety:

Mr. _____

YOU ARE NOW SEATED IN THE CHAMBER OF REFLECTION, WHERE, IN SILENCE AND SOLITUDE, YOU WILL HAVE OPPORTUNITY FOR MEDITATION.

YOU ARE HERE BECAUSE YOU DESIRE TO ENTER THE REALM OF FREEMASONRY. THESE DEGREES WILL INCULCATE THE CARDINAL VIRTUES, AS WELL AS THE PRINCIPLE TENETS OF OUR ORDER. YOU ARE IN THIS CHAMBER TO GIVE YOU A FEW MINUTES TO REFLECT ON WHY YOU ARE HERE FROM YOUR OWN PERSONAL PERSPECTIVE. REFLECT ON THE EXPECTATIONS YOU HAVE, THE BENEFITS YOU HAVE TO GAIN AND CONTRIBUTIONS YOU CAN OFFER THE LODGE IN RETURN.

WHILE THE WORLD IS SHUT OUT, MEDITATE UPON THESE THINGS, AND PREPARE YOUR HEART FOR THE SOLEMN CEREMONIES THROUGH WHICH YOU WILL BE CALLED TO PASS. THERE LIES ON THE TABLE BEFORE

YOU A MELANCHOLY MEMENTO OF MORTALITY. BESIDE IT IS AN HOUR GLASS, WHICH I NOW REVERSE. *(Done.)* AS YOU BEHOLD ITS SLOWLY-FALLING SANDS, LEARN THAT SO SURELY ARE THE WASTING SANDS OF YOUR MORTAL LIFE RUNNING OUT TO DEATH.

THERE IS ALSO ON THIS TABLE THE HOLY BIBLE, WHICH IS OPENED TO PSALM 133. I ENJOIN UPON YOU AT THIS TIME THE READING OF THE VERSES INCLUSIVE OF THAT CHAPTER. WHEN YOU SHALL HAVE CONCLUDED THE READING YOU WILL DISCOVER SOME QUESTIONS, TO WHICH YOUR EXPLICIT ANSWERS ARE REQUIRED IN WRITING. REFLECT ON THEM, AND THEN ANSWER EACH WITH A SIMPLE "YES" OR "NO," ACCORDING TO THE DICTATES OF YOUR CONSCIENCE. THEN SIGN YOUR NAME, IN FULL, TO EACH OF THEM.

YOU ALSO FIND THAT THERE ARE SOME ARTICLES OF CLOTHING, YOU WILL REMOVE ALL METALLIC SUBSTANCES ABOUT YOUR PERSON, REMOVE YOUR CLOTHING AND PUT ON WHAT IS PROVIDED FOR YOU.

I AM NOW ABOUT TO LEAVE YOU ALONE, AND WILL SIGNAL MY DEPARTURE BY THREE KNOCKS UPON THE DOOR, HEARING THEM, YOU WILL REMOVE THE HOODWINK AND PROCEED AS I HAVE DIRECTED. WHEN YOU SHALL HAVE CONCLUDED, GIVE THREE KNOCKS AND I WILL ATTEND YOU.

Appendix B

The following is a translated Fellowcraft Chamber of Reflection Ritual in its entirety:

Mr. _____

> YOU ARE NOW SEATED IN THE CHAMBER OF REFLECTION, WHERE, IN SILENCE AND SOLITUDE, YOU WILL HAVE OPPORTUNITY FOR MEDITATION.
>
> YOU ARE HERE BECAUSE YOU DESIRE TO ENTER THE REALM OF FREEMASONRY. THESE DEGREES WILL INCULCATE THE CARDINAL VIRTUES, AS WELL AS THE PRINCIPLE TENETS OF OUR ORDER. YOU ARE IN THIS CHAMBER TO GIVE YOU A FEW MINUTES TO REFLECT ON WHY YOU ARE HERE FROM YOUR OWN PERSONAL PERSPECTIVE. REFLECT ON THE EXPECTATIONS YOU HAVE, THE BENEFITS YOU HAVE TO GAIN AND CONTRIBUTIONS YOU CAN OFFER THE LODGE IN RETURN.
>
> WHILE THE WORLD IS SHUT OUT, MEDITATE UPON THESE THINGS, AND PREPARE YOUR HEART FOR THE SOLEMN CEREMONIES THROUGH WHICH YOU WILL BE CALLED TO PASS. THERE LIES ON THE TABLE BEFORE

YOU A MELANCHOLY MEMENTO OF MORTALITY. BESIDE IT IS AN HOUR GLASS, WHICH I NOW REVERSE. *(Done.)* AS YOU BEHOLD ITS SLOWLY-FALLING SANDS, LEARN THAT SO SURELY ARE THE WASTING SANDS OF YOUR MORTAL LIFE RUNNING OUT TO DEATH.

THERE IS ALSO ON THIS TABLE THE HOLY BIBLE, WHICH IS OPENED TO AMOS 7. I ENJOIN UPON YOU AT THIS TIME THE READING OF THE VERSES INCLUSIVE OF THAT CHAPTER.

YOU ALSO FIND THAT THERE ARE SOME ARTICLES OF CLOTHING, YOU WILL REMOVE ALL METALLIC SUBSTANCES ABOUT YOUR PERSON, REMOVE YOUR CLOTHING AND PUT ON WHAT IS PROVIDED FOR YOU.

I AM NOW ABOUT TO LEAVE YOU ALONE, AND WILL SIGNAL MY DEPARTURE BY THREE KNOCKS UPON THE DOOR, HEARING THEM, YOU WILL REMOVE THE HOODWINK AND PROCEED AS I HAVE DIRECTED. WHEN YOU SHALL HAVE CONCLUDED, GIVE THREE KNOCKS AND I WILL ATTEND YOU.

Appendix C

The following is a translated Master Mason's

Chamber of Reflection Ritual in its entirety:

BROTHER. _____

YOU ARE NOW SEATED IN THE CHAMBER OF REFLECTION, WHERE, IN SILENCE AND SOLITUDE, YOU WILL HAVE OPPORTUNITY FOR MEDITATION.

YOU ARE HERE BECAUSE YOU DESIRE TO ENTER THE REALM OF FREEMASONRY. THIS DEGREES WILL INCULCATE ALL VIRTUES OF THIS ORGANIZATION, AS WELL AS THE PRINCIPLE TENETS OF OUR ORDER. YOU ARE IN THIS CHAMBER TO GIVE YOU A FEW MINUTES TO REFLECT ON WHY YOU ARE HERE FROM YOUR OWN PERSONAL PERSPECTIVE. REFLECT ON THE EXPECTATIONS YOU HAVE, THE BENEFITS YOU HAVE TO GAIN AND CONTRIBUTIONS YOU CAN OFFER THE LODGE IN RETURN. THIS DEGREE REMINDS THAT WE ARE MORTAL AND THAT ONE DAY, WE WILL CEASE TO EXIST.

WHILE THE WORLD IS SHUT OUT, MEDITATE UPON THESE THINGS, AND PREPARE YOUR

HEART FOR THE SOLEMN CEREMONIES THROUGH WHICH YOU WILL BE CALLED TO PASS. THERE LIES ON THE TABLE BEFORE YOU A MELANCHOLY MEMENTO OF MORTALITY. BESIDE IT IS AN HOUR GLASS, WHICH I NOW REVERSE. *(Done.)* AS YOU BEHOLD ITS SLOWLY-FALLING SANDS, LEARN THAT SO SURELY ARE THE WASTING SANDS OF YOUR MORTAL LIFE RUNNING OUT TO DEATH.

THERE IS ALSO ON THIS TABLE THE HOLY BIBLE, WHICH IS OPENED TO ECCLESIASTES CHAPTER 12. I ENJOIN UPON YOU AT THIS TIME THE READING OF THE VERSES INCLUSIVE OF THAT CHAPTER. WHEN YOU SHALL HAVE CONCLUDED THE READING YOU WILL DISCOVER YOUR LAST WILL AND TESTAMENT. REFLECT ON THIS, AND THEN COMPLETE IT ACCORDING TO THE DICTATES OF YOUR CONSCIENCE. THEN SIGN YOUR NAME, IN FULL.

YOU ALSO FIND THAT THERE ARE SOME ARTICLES OF CLOTHING, YOU WILL REMOVE ALL METALLIC SUBSTANCES ABOUT YOUR PERSON, REMOVE YOUR CLOTHING AND PUT ON WHAT IS PROVIDED FOR YOU.

I AM NOW ABOUT TO LEAVE YOU ALONE, AND WILL SIGNAL MY DEPARTURE BY THREE KNOCKS UPON THE DOOR, HEARING THEM, YOU WILL REMOVE THE HOODWINK AND PROCEED AS I HAVE DIRECTED. WHEN YOU SHALL HAVE CONCLUDED, GIVE THREE KNOCKS AND I WILL ATTEND YOU.

Appendix D

A Chamber of Reflection in Mexico

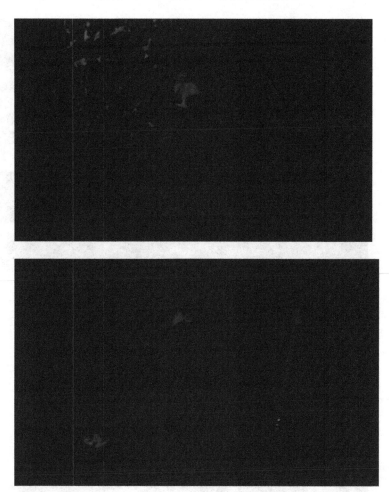

Appendix E

A Chamber of Reflection in the USA

Appendix F

A diagram of a Chamber of Reflection

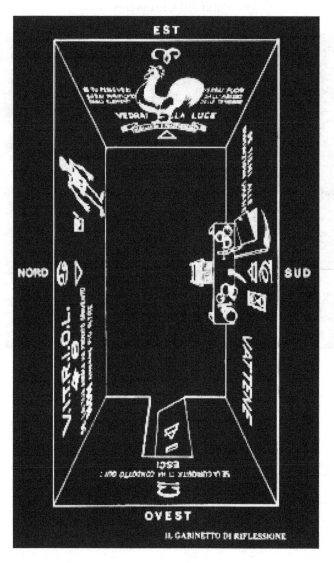

Appendix G

Chamber of Reflection Courtesy of Edolon House / The Joe and Jill Chronicles

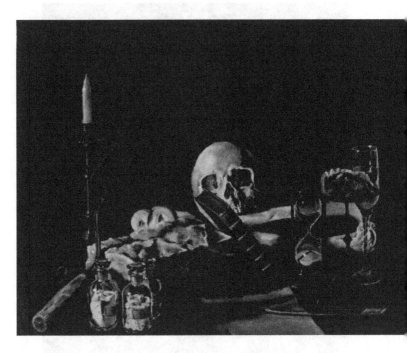

Appendix H

Grand Masters of Colorado Decision on Chambers of Reflection

Decision of the Grand Master

January 23, 2013

Masonic Practices and Observances - The issue has arisen regarding whether practices such as chambers of reflection, processions of officers and brethren into or out of a Lodge room prior to and following the closing of a Lodge, and chains of union are appropriate. Many Lodges in Colorado have been experimenting with such observances in an attempt to enhance their Masonic experience and improve the value and attractiveness of Lodge meetings.

Some have raised objections to these practices, voicing various objections. These practices do not constitute "innovations in the body of Masonry," as some have asserted. Nor are they the "property" of other appendant and concordant organizations.

Therefore, it is my Decision that practices to include, but not be limited to, chambers of reflection, processions of officers and brethren into and out of a Lodge room, and chains of union are authorized in the Grand Lodge of Colorado. Indeed, these practices and similar observances are to be encouraged, as they dignify and adorn the Masonic experience of our brethren. They are to be decidedly Masonic in content, character or style. In order not to conflict with the ritual as authorized by the Custodians of the Work, these embellishments are to be conducted prior to the opening gavel rap or after the closing gavel rap of a Lodge meeting. Were the Custodians of the Work to revise the ritual at some future date to include any such practices or observances, and the Grand Lodge were to adopt such revisions, such would become a part of the approved ritual.

Given under my Hand and Seal of The Most Worshipful Grand Lodge of Ancient Free and Accepted Masons of Colorado this 22nd day of January, A.D. 2013, A.L. 6013.

Fraternally,

Karl J. Hinkle

Karl J. Hinkle
Grand Master

NOTES

1   Dan Brown, *The Lost Symbol* (New York: Doubleday, 2009), 149-160.

2   Daniel Beresniak, *Symbols of Freemasonry* (London: Assouline, 2000), 22-25; Allen Roberts, *The Craft and Its Symbols* (Richmond: Macoy), 13; "Initiation," *Coil's Masonic Encyclopedia* (Richmond: Macoy, 1995)327.

3   Albert Pike, *The Porch and the Middle Chamber* (Kessinger Publishing), 5-13; Christopher Hodapp, *Deciphering the Lost Symbol*   (Berkley: Ulysses press, 2010), 72-73.

4   Giordano Gamberini, *Codice Massonico Delle Logge Riunite E Rettificate Di Francia* (Foggia: Bastogi, 1778), 16-51; Daniel   Beresniak, *Les Symboles de Francs-Macons* (Paris: Assouline, 1997), 24-30.

5   Cliff Porter, *The Secret Psychology of Freemasonry* (Colorado Springs: Starr Publishing, 2011), 128-170; Andrew Hammer,   *Observing the Craft* (Mindhive Books, 2010), 101-102.

6   "Skull and Crossbones," *Coil's Masonic Encyclopedia* (Richmond: Macoy, 1995),623; Hodapp, *Deciphering,*. 52-53,72-73; Porter, *Secret Psychology*, 128-170; Mark O'Connell, and Raje Airey, The Complete Encyclopedia of Signs & Symbols (Hermes House),   159; Hammer, *Observing the Craft*, 100-110.

7   "Hourglass," *Coil's Masonic Encyclopedia* (Richmond: Macoy, 1995), 623; Hodapp, *Deciphering,*,72-73; Porter, *Secret Psychology*, 128-170; *Monitor of the Lodge, Grand Lodge of Texas, A.F. & A.M.* (Waco, TX: Waco Printing Co., 2010), 85;   Hammer, *Observing the Craft*, 100-110; O'Connell and Airey, Signs & Symbols,159, 229 .

8   "Communion," *Coil's Masonic Encyclopedia* (Richmond: Macoy, 1995), 143; Hodapp, *Deciphering,*,72-73; Porter, *Secret Psychology*, 128-170; Hammer, *Observing the Craft*, 100-110.

9   Beresniak, *Symbols of Freemasonry*, 22-25.

10   Lewis Spence, *The Encyclopedia of the Occult* (London: Bracken Books, 1988), 9-13; Hammer, *Observing the Craft*, 100-110;   Hodapp, *Deciphering,*,72-73; Beresniak, *Symbols of Freemasonry*, 22-25; Porter, *Secret Psychology*, 128-170; Beresniak, *Les   Symboles de Francs-Macons*, 24-30; O'Connell and Airey, Signs & Symbols,146-147, 206 .

11   Lewis Spence, *The Encyclopedia of the Occult* (London: Bracken Books, 1988), 9-13; Hammer, *Observing the Craft*, 100-110;   Hodapp, *Deciphering,*,72-73; Beresniak, *Symbols of Freemasonry*, 22-25; Porter, *Secret Psychology*, 128-170;

Beresniak, *Les Symboles de Francs-Macons,* 24-30; O'Connell and Airey, Signs & Symbols,146-147, 206

12   Lewis Spence, *The Encyclopedia of the Occult* (London: Bracken Books, 1988), 9-13; Hammer, *Observing the Craft,* 100-110;   Hodapp, *Deciphering,,*72-73; Beresniak, *Symbols of Freemasonry,* 22-25; Porter, *Secret Psychology,* 128-170; Beresniak, *Les Symboles de Francs-Macons,* 24-30; O'Connell and Airey, Signs & Symbols,146-147, 206

13   M*anual de Aaprendiz Macom Segundo o Ssistema do Rito Brasilero.* (Brasilia: Grande Oriente do Brasil, 1986) ; Hodapp, *Deciphering,,*72-73; Beresniak, *Symbols of Freemasonry,* 22-25; Porter, *Secret Psychology,* 128-170; Hammer, *Observing the Craft,* 100-110; Beresniak, *Les Symboles de Francs-Macons,* 24-30.

14   M. O'Connell and R. Airey, Signs & Symbols,144-147, 206 ,227-233, 240-244; Hodapp, *Deciphering,,*72-73; Beresniak, *Symbols of Freemasonry,* 22-25; Porter, *Secret Psychology,* 128-170; Hammer, *Observing the Craft,* 100-110; Beresniak, *Les Symboles de Francs-Macons,* 24-30 .

15   Gamberini, *Codice Massonico,*16-65; Hodapp, *Deciphering,.*72-73; Beresniak, *Symbols of Freemasonry,* 22-25; Porter, *Secret Psychology,* 128-170; Hammer, *Observing the Craft,* 100-110; Beresniak, *Les Symboles de Francs-Macons,* 24-30; O'Connell and Airey, Signs & Symbols, 92-95, 234 .

16   Gamberini, *Codice Massonico,*16-65; Hodapp, *Deciphering,,*72-73; Beresniak, *Symbols of Freemasonry,* 22-25; Porter, *Secret Psychology,* 128-170; Hammer, *Observing the Craft,* 100-110; Beresniak, *Les Symboles de Francs-Macons,* 24-30; "Chamber of Reflection," *Coil's Masonic Encyclopedia* (Richmond: Macoy, 1995),127; "Chamber of Reflection," Albert G. Mackey, *An Encyclopedia of Freemasonry,* ed., rev. and enl. By Robert L. Clegg, 2 vols (Chicago: Masonic History, 1929), 1 190; "Chamber of Reflection," Robert Macoy, *A Dictionary of Freemasonry*(New York: Gramercy Books, 1989), 106 .

17   *Jachin and Boaz* (London: W. N. Coll, 1762); Perau, M. L'abbei, *L'Ordre des Francs-Macons Trahi, et Le Secret des Mopses Revele'*(AAnsterdam, 1745).

18   S. Brent Morris, *The Folgers Manuscript,* (Illinois: The Masonic Book Club, 1992) 179-200, *xv-xxviii*; Stephen Dafoe, *Morgan* (New Orleans: A Cornerstone Book, 2009)45-124.

19   Dafoe, *Morgan,* 45-124; Morris, *Folgers Manuscript,* 1992.

20   Arturo De Hoyos & Brent Morris, *Committed to the Flames* (London: Lewis Masonic, 2008), 181-186, 193-195.

21   *Grand Masters Decision, Grand Lodge of Colorado* (Appendix H).

171

22   *The Laws of the Grand Lodge of Texas, A.F. & A.M.* (Waco, TX: Waco Printing Co., 2011).

*This was written prior to the edict issued by Grand Master Rogers of the Grand Lodge of Texas in 2013.

Chapter Five
Masonic Labor

"Masonic Labor is to learn and to teach others". I mentioned earlier how this phrase changed my world. In 2007, I started attending Masonic Week in Washington D.C., a weeklong gathering where several national invitational bodies have their annual meeting. The first time I attended, I was not a member of any of the invitational bodies that met there. However, Adoniram Council of the Allied Masonic Degrees has its annual Table Council during Masonic Week, and I was invited to attend it since I was doing research on Table Lodges. I knew very few people that were attending Masonic Week, but I was encouraged to attend for the whole week, which I did. One of the first people I recognized was Rex R. Hutchens, author of *A Bridge to Light*. I had never met him before, but I recognized him from his picture in the book. I was a little star struck to be honest, and I guess I must have been staring because he pointed at me and called me over. Rex told me to have a seat next to him, and asked me "Why are you a Mason?" As I started to give him my answer, he interrupted me to say, "Well did you find what you were looking for?" To which I answered, No. His response was, "Of course you didn't, because you are not doing it right. You have to question everything in Masonry, and you have to question those who claim they know the answers. Masonic Labor is to learn and to teach others. We have to accurately pass on our knowledge in order to be true workers of the craft."

I had never met this man before, yet he saw an imperfect ashlar and wanted to help form it. I spend the rest of that week sitting in the lobby of the Hotel Washington, smoking cigars and drinking White Zinfandel, and absorbing the wisdom of a man whose books I had read. I learned so much that week, and from that day I made it my quest to find what I was looking for in Freemasonry, and to make sure to share that wisdom to future generations of Freemasons.

It is imperative to trade what we have with someone else. Traditions like the ones mentioned in the previous chapters, have become obscure and mostly unknown because that knowledge was not communicated accurately to new generations. Throughout history, there has been so much extremely valuable wisdom lost for centuries. In fact, part of the reasons Western Europe plunged into the Dark Age after the fall of the Roman Empire was because all of the tactic knowledge on how to build and maintain a civilization was locked inside the heads of the Romans – they did not write it down, because none of them were scribes. Therefore, when they died, all that wisdom died with them and it was lost forever. It took

Europe over 1,000 years to relearn all of that wisdom. I am not advocating writing down our rituals or secrets. I am advocating teaching it correctly and passing down the wisdom. There is a difference between wisdom, and information. There is superfluous means of getting information, most search engines such as Google or Bing, can put this information at your fingertips. However, wisdom is not the same thing as information. Wisdom is that information, coupled with experience and context. Which is exactly how Masonry was intended to be passed down; from mouth to ear. Wisdom is information that one can actually use.

The greatest example I can give you of this, is in our rituals. I can name you dozens, if not hundreds of Masons that are amazing with the ritual. They know it forwards, backwards and can do hours of ritual without making a mistake. However, you ask those same Masons to tell you the meaning behind a certain aspect of the ritual, and you might as well be speaking a different language to them. Some might give you the answer they were given by their teacher, or they make up their own. Unfortunately, this creates a snowball effect of misinformation being passed down for generations. Allow me to tell you a story.

> A bunch of parrots in a jungle overhear an explorer telling a joke. The parrots pass this joke on to the next generation of parrots, who pass it on to the next, and so forth. But of course none of the parrots ever actually understand the joke. It keeps on being passed along from parrot to parrot until another explorer come through, hears a parrot tell it, and has a good laugh.

> The original explorer would be delighted to learn that his joke had provided a laugh to a kindred spirit so many years later. However, to the parrots, the laughter is just disruptive: "We are trying to teach this creature the sacred sequence of sounds passed down to us by our fore-parrots, and instead of repeating the sound back to us properly, it is making strange hyena noises. Perhaps this creature has a learning disability."

Even though we memorize ritual, it is crucial that we memorize it as explorers and not as parrots. The genius of the structure of Freemasonry is that, in a worst-case scenario, a lodge of parrots can preserve the mysteries of

Freemasonry until an explorer knocks at the West Gate. Indeed, sadly, that is often how we have survived. A good parrot is considerably superior to a bad parrot in this regard. However, the light of Freemasonry is for the explorers alone. Masonic transmission happens by a process that is a superset of parroting. The ritual must be memorized, and memorized accurately. But if it crackles and sparkles with Masonic light, because the ritualist understands the ritual as an explorer and not as a parrot, then true initiation can take place. Even still, it is up to the candidate to choose to receive the light as an explorer and not as a parrot.

Which brings us to our next topic, what do the words you took while kneeling at the altar mean to you? How far will you go to fulfill your obligation you took at the altar? Those words we as Freemasons recited at our mother lodge, are what binds us together as brothers. Those words are what lets us know that any member of the fraternity will always be looking out for us. That obligation does not have an expiration date. We don't get to pretend it wont apply to us because we have reached a higher offices, such as Worshipful Master or Grand Master. He, who is highest in rank, should be highest in service. The higher you go up the chain of command, the higher your service should be.

That obligation stands for every single Mason. Every Mason, weather he has been honored, or achieved higher rank within the fraternity should follow it. My obligations binds me to my brothers, and I should always be ready to assist those in need. Even if it shall be in at mid night, or barefooted.

I know it may have seemed like I have been critical of several aspects of the fraternity. It may have looked like I might have been attacking or criticizing certain lodges or grand lodges in particular. I explained from the beginning that my job was not to get you to like me, my job was to make you think. My intent was never to shame any lodges, my intent is to prevent Masonry to be taken out of Freemasonry. To motivate you to try to resist the change and restore your own lodge, to the splendor and glory it should be.

So let me leave you with this... Will we become an organization that reveres our past, but does not practice it? Are we good custodians of the mysteries? Do we - "Keep Sacred and inviolable the mysteries of the Order, as these are to distinguish you from the rest of the community, and mark your consequence among Masons." Or have we doomed ourselves to become an institution that promises light, knowledge and esoteric studies, but has long been in darkness.

That is for you to decide, it is up to you to see if we can actually live up to our reputation and deliver to our brothers what he have promised them. It is time we give our members what they most desire. The best way of delivering is by giving them an experience they will remember and cherish, a True Masonic Experience.

Chapter Six
Miscellanea

This is a collection of useful information that may be used for different aspects of your lodge. They all are either part of the public domain or under copyright of the author.

MASONIC EMBLEMS

Respectfully Dedicated by permission to J. F. Lloyd, Melville Esq.e of Branxby, The Most Worshipful Grand Master Mason of Scotland. By His Humble Servant William Gray

Masonic Dates and Calendars

In order to understand and make a correct timeline of Masonic lessons one needs to learn the distinction and definitions of the "Masonic Dates"

A.L.   *Anno Lucius* – In the year of Light

A.I.   *Anno Inventionis* - In the year of Discovery

A.B.   *Anno Benedictionis* - In the year of Blessing

A.D.   *Anno Depositionis* – In the year of the Deposit

A.O.   *Anno Ordinis* – In the year of the Order

A.M.   *Anno Mundi* – In the year of the World

In the common time, we use BC & AD to label or number the years in the Julian and Gregorian calendars. BC refers to *Before Christ* as in before Christ was born. AD refers to *Anno Domini*, which in Latin it means in the year of our Lord. Therefore, the Year 1AD is the first year of Christ's life.

Ancient Craft Masons date from the creation of the world. *Anno Lucius (A.L)* adds 4000 to the common time, so the year 2015 becomes 6015.

Royal Arch Masons date from the completion off the second temple by Zerubbabel. *Anno Inventionis* (A.I.) adds 530 to the common time, so the year 2015 becomes 2545.

Royal and Select Masters date from the completion of the Temple of Solomon. *Anno Depositionis* (A.D.) adds 1000 to the common time, so the year 2015 becomes 3015. It is important not to confuse *Anno Depositionis* with *Anno Domini* since the acronym for both is AD.

Knights Templar date from the organization of their Order. *Anno Ordinis* (A.O.) deducts 1,118 from the common time, so the year 2015 becomes 897.

The Scottish Rite date is the same as the Ancient Craft Masons, except for the use of the Jewish Chronology. *Anno Mundi (A.M.)* adds 3760 to the common time, so the year 2015 becomes 5775.

The Order of High Priesthood date from the blessing of Abraham by Melchizedek, High Priest & King of Salem. *Anno Benedictionis* (A.B.) adds 1930 to the common time, so the year 2015 becomes 3945.

A Toast to the Flag

Here's to the red of it -
There's not a thread of it,
No, nor a shred of it
In all the spread of it
From foot to head.
But heroes bled for it,
Faced steel and lead for it,
Precious blood shed for it,
Bathing it red!

Here's to the white of it -
Thrilled by the sight of it.
Who knows the right of it,
But feels the might of it
Through day and night?
Womanhood's care for it
Made manhood dare for it.
Purity's prayer for it
Keeps it so white.

Here's to the blue of it -
Beauteous view of it,
Heavenly hue of it,
Star-spangled dew of it
Constant and true.
Diadems gleam for it,
States stand supreme for it,
Liberty's beam for it
Brightens the blue!

Here's to the whole of it -
Stars, stripes and pole of it.
Body and soul of it,
O, and the roll of it,

Sun shining through.
Hearts in accord for it,
Thanking the Lord for it,
Red, White and Blue!

The Ceremony of Introducing a
Intended Brother into the Lodge

Red Skelton's Pelage to the Flag

The following words were spoken by a famous Freemason, the late Red Skelton on his television program as he related the story of his teacher, Mr. Laswell, who felt his students had come to think of the Pledge of Allegiance as merely something to recite in class each day.

Now, more than ever, listen to the meaning of these words.

"I've been listening to you boys and girls recite the Pledge of Allegiance all semester

and it seems as though it is becoming monotonous to you.

If I may, may I recite it and try to explain to you the meaning of each word?"

I

me, an individual, a committee of one.

Pledge

dedicate all of my worldly goods to give without self pity.

Allegiance

my love and my devotion.

To the flag

our standard, Old Glory, a symbol of freedom. Wherever

she waves, there's respect because your loyalty has given

her a dignity that shouts freedom is everybody's job!

United

that means that we have all come together.

States

individual communities that have united into 48 great states.

Forty-eight individual communities with pride and dignity and

purpose; all divided with imaginary boundaries, yet united to

a common purpose, and that's love for country.

And to the republic

a state in which sovereign power is

invested in representatives chosen by the

people to govern. And government is the people

and it's from the people to the leaders, not from

the leaders to the people.

For which it stands, one nation

one nation, meaning "so

blessed by God"

Indivisible

incapable of being divided.

With liberty

which is freedom -- the right of power to live one's

own life without threats, fear or some sort of

retaliation.

And Justice

the principle or quality of dealing fairly with others.

For all

which means, boys and girls, it's as much your

country as it is mine.

Since I was a small boy, two states have been added to our country

and two words have been added to the pledge of Allegiance...

UNDER GOD

Wouldn't it be a pity if someone said

that is a prayer

and that would be eliminated from schools too?

God Bless America!

The manner of Receiving the word from the
MASTER

Masonic Structure

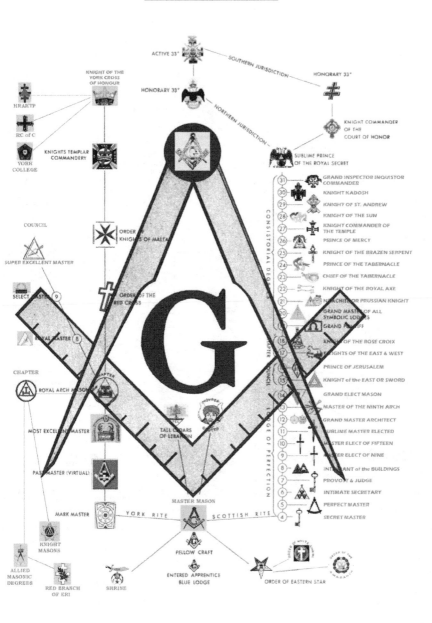

ACTIVE 33°
SOUTHERN JURISDICTION
HONORARY 33°

KNIGHT OF THE
YORK CROSS
OF HONOUR

HONORARY 33°

NORTHERN JURISDICTION

HKARTP

KNIGHT COMMANDER
OF THE
COURT OF HONOR

RC of C

YORK
COLLEGE

KNIGHTS TEMPLAR
COMMANDERY

SUBLIME PRINCE
OF THE ROYAL SECRET

(31) GRAND INSPECTOR INQUISTOR
COMMANDER
(30) KNIGHT KADOSH
(29) KNIGHT OF ST. ANDREW
(28) KNIGHT OF THE SUN
(27) KNIGHT COMMANDER OF
THE TEMPLE
(26) PRINCE OF MERCY
(25) KNIGHT OF THE BRAZEN SERPENT
(24) PRINCE OF THE TABERNACLE
(23) CHIEF OF THE TABERNACLE
(22) KNIGHT OF THE ROYAL AXE
(21) NOACHITE OR PRUSSIAN KNIGHT
(20) GRAND MASTER OF ALL
SYMBOLIC LODGES
(19) GRAND PONTIFF
(18) KNIGHT OF THE ROSE CROIX
(17) KNIGHTS OF THE EAST & WEST
(16) PRINCE OF JERUSALEM
(15) KNIGHT of the EAST OR SWORD
(14) GRAND ELECT MASON
(13) MASTER OF THE NINTH ARCH
(12) GRAND MASTER ARCHITECT
(11) SUBLIME MASTER ELECTED
(10) MASTER ELECT OF FIFTEEN
(9) MASTER ELECT OF NINE
(8) INTENDANT of the BUILDINGS
(7) PROVOST & JUDGE
(6) INTIMATE SECRETARY
(5) PERFECT MASTER
(4) SECRET MASTER

COUNCIL

ORDER OF
KNIGHTS OF MALTA

SUPER EXCELLENT MASTER

SELECT MASTER (9)

ORDER OF THE
RED CROSS

ROYAL MASTER (8)

CHAPTER

ROYAL ARCH MASON

MOST EXCELLENT MASTER

TALL CEDARS
OF LEBANON

PAST MASTER (VIRTUAL)

MARK MASTER

YORK RITE

MASTER MASON

SCOTTISH RITE

KNIGHT
MASONS

FELLOW CRAFT

ALLIED
MASONIC
DEGREES

RED BRANCH
OF ERI

SHRINE

ENTERED APPRENTICE
BLUE LODGE

ORDER OF EASTERN STAR

CONSISTORIAL DEGREES

CHAPTER

COUNCIL

LODGE OF PERFECTION

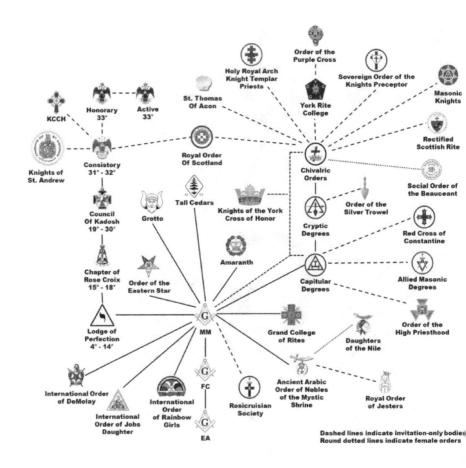

KCCH

Honorary 33°

Active 33°

St. Thomas Of Acon

Order of the Purple Cross

Holy Royal Arch Knight Templar Priests

York Rite College

Sovereign Order of the Knights Preceptor

Masonic Knights

Knights of St. Andrew

Consistory 31° - 32°

Royal Order Of Scotland

Chivalric Orders

Rectified Scottish Rite

Social Order of the Beaucesant

Council Of Kadosh 19° - 30°

Grotto

Tall Cedars

Knights of the York Cross of Honor

Order of the Silver Trowel

Cryptic Degrees

Red Cross of Constantine

Chapter of Rose Croix 15° - 18°

Order of the Eastern Star

Amaranth

Capitular Degrees

Allied Masonic Degrees

Lodge of Perfection 4° - 14°

G MM

Grand College of Rites

Daughters of the Nile

Order of the High Priesthood

International Order of DeMolay

International Order of Jobs Daughter

International Order of Rainbow Girls

G FC

Rosicruisian Society

Ancient Arabic Order of Nobles of the Mystic Shrine

Royal Order of Jesters

G EA

Dashed lines indicate invitation-only bodies
Round dotted lines indicate female orders

Masonic Dictionary

A

ABIF: Meaning is "his father".

ADMONISH: T o caution, advise, or counsel against; to express warning or disapproval; to give friendly, earnest advice and encouragement.

ADONAI: The lord.

ADVANCE: Going from one degree to the next after showing proficiency in the preceding degree.

ADVERSE BALLOT: In case the ballot on a petition for the degrees or for affiliation is adverse, the Master may, if he so desires, spread the ballot again to make certain no error occurred. In so doing, he should state his reason for the second spreading.

A.E.O.N.M.S.: Ancient Egyptian Order Nobles Mystic Shrine (Prince Hall Shrine).

AGREEABLY: In conformity with.

ALLEGORICAL: An allegory is a story told through symbols, or an idea so expressed.

ALLEGORY: Analogy or comparison; a story told to illustrate a principle. It comes from the Greek meaning "to say something different."

ALL SEEING-EYE: An emblem reminding us that we are constantly in God's presence.

ALPHA and OMEGA: First and last Greek letters of the alphabet. The beginning and the end of all things; the first and the last, often mentioned in the Scriptures and in several of the Masonic degrees.

AMEN: From the Hebrew meaning "verily, truly, certainly." One person confirms the words of another. Masonically, answered by "So mote it be."

ANCIENT: Old, time honored.

ANNO BENEFACIO: (A.B.) Latin for "In the Year of the Blessing." Used by the Order of High Priesthood for dating their documents. (1930 added to the current date.)

ANNO DEPOSITIONIS: (A.Dep.) Latin for "In the Year of the Deposit. "The Cryptic Masonic date designation. (Add 1000 to the current date.)

ANNO DOMINI: (A.D.) Latin for "Year of our Lord."

ANNO INVENTIONIS: (A.I.) Latin meaning "In the Year of Discovery." The Royal Arch date designation. (Add 530 to the current date.)

ANNO LUCIS: (A.L.) Latin meaning "In the Year of Light, "the date used by Ancient Craft Masonry. (Add 4000 to the current date.)

ANNO MUNDI: (A.M.) Latin meaning "In the Year of the World." The date used by the Scottish Rite. (Add 3760 to the current year until September; if after September, add 3761.

ANNO ORDINIS: (A.O.) L thin meaning "In the Year of e Order." The date used by the Knights Templar. (Subtracts 1118 from the current date.)

ANOINT: To apply oil to, or pour oil on, particularly holy oil as a sign of elevation to kingship or consecration to priesthood. Hence, "anointed," one accepted by the Lord, as "The Lord's anointed." . Comes from the custom of the Egyptians and Jews.

APPRENTICE: Comes from the Latin word apprehendre meaning "to grasp to master a thing" Hence the leaner

APRON: The badge of a Mason. Originally among priesthoods as a badge of office and a means of ornamentation. The Masonic apron should be white lambskin. It should be presented to the candidate at his initiation and not at some subsequent time. No substitute should be used. From the French word napron meaning "an apron of cloth." From earliest times in Persia, Egypt, India, the Jewish Essenes, the white apron was a badge of honor and candidates were invested with it, or a sash, or a robe. Its reference is to purity of heart, to innocence of conduct.

ARCHITECT: One who designs buildings.

ARCHITECTURE: The art or science of building.

ARCHIVES: a place for the safe keeping of records ; the records themselves.

ARTIFICER: a craftsman or skilled laborer: one who makes beautiful objects.

ARTS: branches of learning, as in the lecture of the F.C. degree. In E.A. degree: skills.

ASHLAR: a block of stone from which a column, capital, or other finished product is carved or hewn.

ASHLAR: A stone as taken from the quarry; an unpolished stone.

ATHEIST: One who does not believe in God.

B

BADE: Told; ordered; requested; directed.

BALLOT: A secret vote made by balls, cubes or in writing.

BEEHIVE: Symbolic of systematized industry. What one may not be able to accomplish alone may be easily performed when all work together at one task.

BENEFICENT: Doing or producing good.

BLAZING STAR: Symbol of light; of Divine direction in the journey through life; symbolizes a true Freemason who, by perfecting himself in the way of truth (knowledge), becomes like a blazing star. In English lodges, symbolizes sun which enlightens the earth, dispensing its blessings to all mankind and giving light and life to all things.

BLUE LODGE. A term which has grown into use over the years meaning the three degrees of the lodge, or Symbolic Masonry. In the early years, Master Masons wore blue lined aprons. Blue is symbolic of perfection, benevolence, truth, universal friendship, fidelity.

BOAZ: Comes from the Hebrew meaning "in strength." The left hand pillar that stood at the porch of King Solomon's Temple.

BOOK OF CONSTITUTIONS: An emblem of law signifying that our moral and spiritual character is grounded in law and order and that no man can live a satisfying life who lives lawlessly.

BOOK OF CONSTITUTIONS GUARDED BY THE TYLER'S SWORD: An admonishment to the Mason that he should be guarded in his words and actions; obedience to the law.

BOOK OF THE LAW: The sacred book which reveals the will of God. To Christians, the Bible; to the Brahman, the Vedas, etc.

BOURNE: Boundaries; limits.

BRAZEN: Made of brass.

BRETHREN: The term is used in speaking of Masons, and in this connection is preferable to "brothers."

BROKEN COLUMN: Columns or pillars were used among the early Hebrews to signify nobles or princes; it is from such that we get the expression "pillar of the church." Masonically, the broken column refers to the fall of one of the chief supporters of the Craft; an untimely death.

C

CABLE TOW: The tie by which the candidate is bound to his brethren; the length of a Mason's cable tow is the scope of his ability to go to the relief of a brother in need. In early years the distance was three miles; in present time it is usually considered about forty miles.

CALENDAR, MASONIC: Masons date their official documents in a manner peculiar to themselves. The various dates for the different bodies are based on important points in history.

CANOPY: a tent-like covering. "Canopy of heaven", the sky.

CARDINAL: Of basic importance; main; primary; essential; principal.

CARDINAL POINTS: East: Wisdom; West: Strength; South: Beauty; North: Darkness.

CARDINAL VIRTUES: Temperance, Fortitude, Prudence, and Justice are virtues of morality as laid down by Plato. Cardinal comes from the Latin cardo meaning "chief or fundamental."

CATECHISM: Instructions of Freemasonry.

CEDARS: Members of the Tall Cedars of Lebanon, a non-Masonic organization composed of Freemasons.

CELESTIAL CANOPY: Symbolic covering of the lodge; heavenly.

CEMENT: Brotherly love binds Freemasons of all countries, races and creeds in one common brotherhood.

CHECKERED FLOOR: The Mosaic Pavement.

CHRISTIAN VIRTUES: Faith, Hope, and Charity.

CHALK, CHARCOAL, AND CLAY: Freedom, fervency, and zeal.

CHAPITERS: the ornamental tops or capitals of pillars.

CHARTER: a document setting forth a set of granted rights and privileges given by the Grand Lodge to the constituent Lodge at the tinic of Constitution. The Master is its custodian, and must see to its security at all times. The charter must be in the Lodge room during all communications of the Lodge, preferably in the Master's charge, but it may be on the Secretary's desk, or in the archives of the Lodge. It should not be framed to hang on the wall. The request of a visitor to inspect the charter in advance be granted or refused. Should the charter be lost or destroyed, the Grand Master or Grand Secretary should be notified at once. Pending the issuing of a duplicate charter, a permission, or dispensation to continue work should be obtained from the Grand Master.

CHASTEN: To correct by discipline.

CIRCLE: A figure which has neither beginning nor end and symbolizes eternity; the universe.

CIRCURNAMBULATION: The movement is in imitation of the apparent course of the sun, and so is in the form of an ellipse.

CIRCUMSCRIBED: literally encircled hence limited. To draw a line around; to limit in range of activity definitely and clearly.

CLAD: Covered or clothed.

CLANDESTINE: not regular.

CLOTHED, PROPERLY: With white gloves and apron, and the jewel of his Masonic rank. Today the gloves are usually dispensed with.

COLUMNS: From the Latin culmen meaning "a pillar to support or adorn a building." In Masonry the symbolic Significance pertains to the supports of a lodge: Wisdom, Strength and Beauty.

COLUMNS, WARDENS: Represent Jachin and Boaz. While the lodge is at work the columns are erect and horizontal, respectively; while on refreshment, such positions are reversed.

COMMUNICATIONS: The meetings of a Symbolic lodge.

COMPASS: A mathematical instrument for dividing and drawing circles; an instrument indicating the magnetic meridian.

COMPASSES: One of the Working Tools. Freemasons have adopted the plural spelling to distinguish it from the magnetic compass.

COMPOSITE: One of the Five Orders of Architecture developed late in the Roman period as an enriched version of the Corinthian that combines the Corinthian and Ionic styles.

CORINTHIAN: One of the three classical (Greek) orders of architecture—the most ornamented of the three. Originated in the city of Corinth in Greece.

CORNICE: The ornamented slab placed above the capital of a pillar, and extending beyond it.

COWANS: profanes, pretenders, intruders, particularly those seeking to obtain the secrets of Masonry unlawfully.

CORNUCOPIA: The horn of plenty; a symbol of abundance.

CORN, WINE, AND OIL: Three elements of consecration. In ancient times these were regarded as the basic commodities for the support of life and constituted the wealth of the people. Today in the U.S. we think of corn as maize, but the original meaning is an edible grain or cereal. The Hebrew word for corn means "to be increased or to multiply."

CUBIT: A n ancient unit of linear measure, approximately 18 inches in today's measure.

D

DAIS: The platform, or raised floor, in the East of the lodge where the Master sits. In the lodge, the steps to this should be three. The Senior Warden's place should be raised two steps and that of the junior Warden, one step.

DARKNESS: Symbolizes that state of ignorance before light (knowledge) is received.

D.D.G.M: District Deputy Grand Master, an assistant who acts for the Grand Master in a particular district.

DEACON: Comes from the Greek diakonos meaning "messenger or waiting-man."

"DEDICATED TO THE MEMORY OF THE HOLY SAINTS JOHN.": Dedication is a less sacred ceremony than consecration. Hence, lodges are consecrated to God, but dedicated to patrons of the Fraternity.

DEMIT or DIMIT: A release; a resignation of membership; a paper certifying a withdrawal from a lodge (or Masonic body) when in good standing. Both spellings are used, although DIMIT is peculiar to Freemasonry only. In the U.S. some jurisdictions use the former spelling, but the majority use the latter, "Dimit."

DESTITUTE: lacking means, as without money or food.

DIGEST: Book of laws of a Grand Lodge in the U.S.; sometimes called The Code.

DISPENSATION: Permission to do that which would be forbidden otherwise.

DISTRESS: Physical or mental anguish. A brother in distress does not necessarily mean that he is without funds.

DIVISTED: To deprive or take away from; to undress or remove clothing, ornaments, or equipment.

DORIC: One of the three classical (Greek) orders of architecture—the oldest and simplest of the three, originated in an area of ancient Greece known as Doris.

DOTAGE: An advanced age when the mind is no longer able to comprehend clearly.

DUE EAST AND WEST: Moses built the Tabernacle due east and west, and this practice was carried on by the church builders. The Freemason travels from the West to the East (light) in search of a Master from whom he may gain instruction, or light,

DUE FORM: A Masonic body is opened or closed in "due form" when performed fully according to a prescribed ritual. Distinguished from "ample form."

DUE GUARD: A mode of recognition peculiar to Freemasons.

DULY AND TRULY PREPARED: That the candidate is truly prepared in his heart

and mind to receive further enlightenment; also, properly clothed, Masonically.

E

EAR, THE ATTENTIVE OR LISTENING: The Hebrew word means not only to hear, but to understand and to obey.

EAST: From the Sun worshipers down through the ages, the East has always been considered the most honored place because the sun rises in the East and is the region from which light rises.

EAVESDROPPER: One who attempts to listen surreptitiously; literally, one standing under the eaves and thus gets only the "droppings."

ECLIPTIC: the imaginary line followed on the earth's surface by the direct ray of the sun during the year. It makes an angle of 23' 27' with the equator. Jerusalem is located in approximately 31' 30' north attitude, that is, approximately 7' 3' north of the ecliptic.

EDIFICE: A building, especially one of imposing appearance or size.

EMBLEM: A representation of an idea by a visible object; a symbolical figure or design.

EMBLEMATICAL: symbolical, representing.

EMBROIDERED: having a border.

EMULATION: Ambitious rivalry; ambition or desire to equal or excel others in achievement

ENGRAVE: To cut figures or letters into wood or metal.

ENTERED APPRENTICE: In Operative Masonry the apprenticeship lasted seven years; if then found acceptable, the apprentice's name was entered on the books of the lodge and he was given a recognized place in the craft organization.

EQUIVOCATION: To avoid committing oneself to what one says; uncertainty; uncertain or questioning disposition of mind.

ETCH: To produce as a pattern on a hard surface by eating into the material's surface as with acid or a laser beam.

EUCLID: the first mathematician to Systematize the science of geometry.

EXAMINATION: the examination of a brother to determine his geniuses should not aim at displaying the committee's knowledge. It is a test of the visitor. He need not be able to answer questions from the Posting Lecture. He should know the signs, grips, and words.

EXPULSION: Forcible ejection from membership for such reasons as un-Masonic conduct, crimes, etc. It is the most severe of Masonic penalties and deprives the person of all rights and privileges formerly enjoyed from his lodge and the Fraternity as a whole.

F

FAITH. The evidence of things not seen; confidence; trust.

FAITHFUL BREAST: Symbolically, the initiate is instructed that the lessons he has received are to be treasured in his heart and remembered, and not to be forgotten; that which is told in confidence will be so held.

FELLOW: A member of a group having common characteristics; an associate; an equal in rank or power or character.

FELLOWCRAFT: A craftsman no longer an apprentice who has been admitted as full member, but who has not yet reached the status of a master. The fellowcraft age represents the stage of manhood.

FEALTY: Loyalty.

FIAT LUX ET LUX FIT: Latin motto meaning "Let there be light, and there was light."

FIDELITY: faithfulness.

FIRST LANDMARKS OF MASONRY: Modes of recognition with no variation.

FORM OF A LODGE: An oblong square or parallelogram, twice as long as wide. At the time of the Temple, the only known world was the Mediterranean Sea and the countries to the north, south and east, forming an oblong. Thus, the Freemason's lodge was the world itself.

47TH PROPOSITION OF EUCLID: Derived its name from the fact that it was the 47th problem in Euclid's geometry. Sometimes called problem or theorem, which are also correct. The 47th Proposition, or problem, is to prove that in a right angled triangle, the sum of the squares of the two sides is equal to the square of the hypotenuse. Masonically, it is an emblem of the arts and sciences and reminds us that next to sinfulness, the most dangerous enemy of life is ignorance.

FORTITUDE: Strength of mind that enables a person to encounter danger, or bear pain or adversity, with courage

FRATERNITY: A brotherhood, in which blood-bonds are replaced by a common devotion to a principle, code, or creed.

FREE BORN: A free soul; one having attained mastery of himself by self discipline. It is a misconception that this refers to one not born into slavery.

FREEMASONS: The early builders in Operative Masonry times were free men, not serfs or bondsmen and were free to move from one place to another as their work demanded. Thus, they came to be called "Freemasons."

FURNISHINGS OF A LODGE: Holy Bible, Square and Compasses, Charter or Dispensation.

G

"G": The letter -G- is the Saxon representative of the Hebrew Yod and the Greek Tau; The initial letter of the name of the Eternal in those languages. It stands not only for God, but for Geometry, that science so important to all Freemasons.

G.A.O.T.U.: Grand Architect of the Universe.

GAVEL: Derives its name from its shape-that of the gable or gavel end of a house. It is a tool used by a stonemason and resembles a hammer having a pointed end for cutting. The Working Tool gavel differs from the upright gavel, or "Hiram." (See Hiram.)

GOD: The Hebrew words for Beauty, Strength, and Wisdom (the supports of Freemasonry) are Gomer, Oz, and Dabar. The initials of these words compose the English name of the Deity.

GRAND EAST: The place where the Grand Lodge holds its communications and from which place the edicts are issued.

GREAT LIGHTS: The Holy Bible, Square and Compasses. The Bible represents the will of God, the Square is the physical life of man and the Compasses represents the moral and spiritual life.

GRIPS: Every brother following his raising should be taught to start with the grip of an Entered Apprentice Mason and go through the grips, passes, and words to the Grand Masonic Word.

GUILD (GILD) MASONS.

GUTTURAL: From the Latin guttur meaning "the throat."

H

HISTORICAL: According to history, verifiable, capable of documentary proof. We also speak of traditional and legendary history, meaning popular belief, not upheld by fact.

HOMAGE: respect, as applied to men; worship, as applied to deity.

HOUR GLASS: Emblem of life.

HEALED: Obligated in a degree which the Mason has not had conferred on him. To "heal" is to "make valid."

HELE: Pronounced "hail" and means to keep guarded, or secret. Sometimes spelled "hale, hail, or hale."

HEMISPHERE: Half of the earth's surface, as the western hemisphere, the northern hemisphere.

HIEROGLYPHICS: Literally the symbols in the priestly writings of the Egyptians. Generally, a symbol or sign the meaning of which is known only to the initiated.

HIRAM: An upright gavel made in the form of a maul and used by a presiding officer.

H.K.T: Hiram, King of Tyre.

HOODWINK: A blindfold which is a symbol of secrecy; mystical darkness.

HOODWINKED: Blindfolded.

HOMAGE: Respect or reverence paid or rendered; expression of high regard

HOUR GLASS: An emblem of the passage of time.

HOUSE NOT MADE WITH HANDS: That which lies beyond death; heaven; the world of spiritual truth (II Corinthians 5:1)

I

ILL. OR ILLUSTRIOUS: A title used in addressing members of the 33rd.

ILLUSTRATE: Giving or showing an example.

ILLUSTRATION: A drawing, picture, or example.

ILLUSTRATIVE: Showing by example or picture.

IMMEMORIAL: Extending or existing since beyond the reach of memory.

IN GOOD STANDING: When dues are current.

INDISCRIMINATELY: Without distinction between.

INITIATIC: Of, or relating to, initiation; possessing a sacred traditional character.

INITIATION: A new undertaking, the beginning of a new, spiritual life, or instruction.

I.N.R.I: Jesus Nazarenus, Rex Iudworum, meaning "Jesus of Nazareth, King of the Jews."

INTELLIGIBLE: Capable of being read or understood

INVIOLATE: Not broken or disregarded; not told to others; respected.

IONIC: One of the three classical (Greek) orders of architecture, originated in an area of ancient Greece known as Ionia.

J

JACHIN: Comes from two Hebrew words meaning "God will establish." The right hand pillar of the porch of King Solomon's Temple.

JACOB'S LADDER: Symbol of progress from earth to heaven.

JEWELS, MOVABLE AND IMMOVABLE: The Movable jewels are the Rough and Perfect Ashlars and the Trestle Board and are so called because they are not confined to any particular part of the lodge whereas the Immovable jewels: the Square, Level, and Plumb, have definite locations. They are called "jewels" not because of their materials, but because of their meaning. The word "jewel" comes from the Greek meaning "bright or shining."

JUDICIOUS: Having, exercising, or characterized by sound judgment; discrete; wise

K

KORAN, THE: The Sacred Volume of Mohammedan Law.

L

LAMB: "In all ages the Lamb has been deemed an emblem of innocence." The candidate is therefore given a white lambskin apron.

LANDMARKS: Ancient and universal customs of the Order which gradually grew into operation as rules of action.

LAWFUL AGE: A man of discretion.

LAWFUL INFORMATION: That one has tested by trial and examination, or knows that such has been done by another.

LEGALLY CONSTITUTED: A Lodge working under proper authority and Charter from a Grand Lodge.

LEGENDARY: according to popular belief or report, but without proof. A legend usually carries with it the idea of the miraculous.

LEGIBLE: Capable of being read.

LIBERAL ARTS AND SCIENCES: Grammar, Rhetoric, Logic, Arithmetic, Geometry, Music, and Astronomy.

LIGHT: Symbolic of knowledge and understanding in Masonry and most traditional societies

LILY-WORK: Emblem of peace and unity.

LODGE OF THE HOLY SAINTS JOHN OF JERUSALEM and LODGE OF ST. JOHN: Masonic tradition has it that the primitive, or mother, Lodge was held at Jerusalem and dedicated to St. John the Baptist, and then to St. John the Evangelist, and finally to both. This Lodge was therefore called "The Lodge of the Holy Saints John of Jerusalem." From this Lodge all other Lodges are supposed, figuratively, to descend.

LOST WORD: That for which the Mason search is to discover the divine in himself and in the world that he might achieve mental satisfaction and ultimate happiness.

LOW TWELVE: The hour of midnight; darkness is a symbol of death as well as of ignorance.

LUX E TENEBRIS: Latin meaning "Light out of darkness."

M

MAKING A MASON "AT SIGHT": By a Grand Master's prerogative, some constitutional requirement is set aside-usually the ballot, and a man is made a Master Mason without waiting or instruction between degrees.

MANUAL: Having to do with, or involving, the hands

MASONIC AGES: The age of an Entered Apprentice is said to be three years (the symbol of peace or perfect harmony); that of a Fellowcraft, five years (the symbol of active life); and that of a Master Mason, seven years (the symbol of perfection).

MERIDIAN: The position of the sun at noon.

MORIAH: A hill in Jerusalem on which the Temple of Solomon was built.

MOSAIC PAVEMENT: Tessellated pavement or checkered floor. An inlay floor composed of black and white squares.

MOUTH TO EAR: The method whereby the esoteric work of Freemasonry is passed on from one Mason to another, or from one Mason to the candidate who is qualified to receive such information.

MYSTIC TIE: Spiritual tie not easily broken; fellowship among Masons.

N

NEITHER NAKED NOR CLOTHED: Neither unclothed, or defenseless, nor clothed and self-sufficient.

NOBLES: Members of the Mystic Shrine.

O

OATH: A solemn affirmation, in the name of God, that what one testifies is true.

OBLIGATION: A promise or pledge of obedience. The Mason takes an obligation, not an oath, that he will not depart from the promises he makes.

OBLONG SQUARE: A right angle with one side longer than the other.

ORALLY: Aloud, spoken.

ORIENTAL CHAIR: The seat of the Master in the East; the Oriental Chair of King Solomon.

ORNAMENTS OF A LODGE: The Mosaic Pavement, Indented Tessel, and Blazing Star.

ORNAN: Name of Jebusite from whom David purchased a thresingfloor in Jerusalem in which King Solomon's temple was built. This was previously the site of the alter.

P

PAST: A term applied in Masonry to an officer who has held an office for the term for which he was elected, and has then retired, as Past Master, Past Senior Grand Warden.

PASSING THE CHAIR: The ceremony of installation of the presiding officer.

PECTORAL: Pertaining to the breast.

PEDAL: Of, or relating to, the foot or feet.

PEDESTALS: The columns before the Master and Wardens of a lodge.

PERFECT AHSLAR: Every Mason is expected to perfect or "polish" himself in building his character in order that he may become acceptable in the sight of God and be fit to take his rightful place in the finished work of Masonry.

PERFECT LODGE: One which contains the constitutional number of members.

PERFECT POINTS OF ENTRANCE: Symbolic action called for on entrance into a lodge.

PERFECT SQUARE: A right angle with the sides equal.

PHARAOH: The title of the ruler of ancient Egypt.

PHILALETHES: Friends of truth.

PLANETARY: Pertaining to the planets.

PLUMB: An instrument for erecting perpendiculars.

PLUMB LINE: The Working Tool of a Past Master; the perfect emblem of uprightness.

POTENTATE: A ruler, sovereign, or monarch.

POT OF INCENSE: Signifies that, of all forms of worship, it is more acceptable to God to be pure and blameless in our inner lives than anything else.

PRECEPTS: A principle or instruction intended especially as a general rule of action.

PROFANE: A non-Mason, The word comes from the Latin pro meaning "before" and Janum meaning "a temple." Hence, in Masonry it means those who have not been in the Temple, that is, initiated.

PROFICIENT: Means not only proficient in the ritualistic work, but before the world in daily living.

PRUDENCE: The ability to govern and discipline oneself by the use of reason; skill and good judgment in the management of affairs or the use of resources; caution or circumspection as to danger or risk

Q

R

REFRESHMENT: Rest period symbolized by noon.

REGULAR LODGE: One working under a charter or warrant from a legal authority.

REPRIMAND: One of the Masonic penalties which can be and is enforced to reprove.

RITE: Derived from the Latin *ritus*, which comes from the Sanskrit *ri*, meaning to flow and usually associated with a running stream or a way. This term is closely linked by its definition with the term tradition and denotes the continuous performance or preservation of something sacred associated with the Divine

RITUAL: Comes from the Latin ritualis meaning "ceremonial forms."

ROUGH ASHLAR: The unenlightened member; man in his natural state before being educated.

S

SANCTUM SANCTORUM: Latin for "Holy of Holies."

SHIBBOLETH: An ear of corn; a test word; a watchword; slogan.

SHOD: Wearing footgear; with shoes on

SIGNS, MASONIC: Modes of recognition often serving as a reminder of some event or pledge.

SOLSTICE: The point in the ecliptic at which the sun is farthest from the equator (north in summer, south in winter).

SONS OF LIGHT: During the building of King Solomon's Temple the Masons were so called.

SPECULATIVE MASONRY: Freemasonry in its modern acceptance; the application of the implements of Operative masonry to a system of ethics.

SPRIG OF ACACIA: Symbolizes the immortality of the soul.

STATIONS AND PLACES: Officers are elected to stations and appointed to places.

SUBDUE: To bring under control, especially by an exertion of the will; to reduce the intensity or degree of; tone down.

SUBLIME: Lofty, grand, or exalted in thought, expression, or manner; of outstanding spiritual, intellectual, or moral worth; tending to inspire awe

SUMMONS: A notification from the Master to appear. For its neglect, because it comes directly under the province of his obligation, a member may be disciplined and/or punished.

SUPERFLUITY: Excess; unnecessary; immoderate, especially living habits or desires.

SUPERFLUOUS: exceeding what is needed; excess; unnecessary.

SUSPENSION: Temporary privation of power or rights, such as suspension for nonpayment of dues. One of the Masonic penalties.

SWORD POINTING TO THE NAKED HEART: Signifies that justice is one of the most rigorous laws and if we are unjust in our hearts, the center of our being, the inevitable result of injustice will find us out.

SYMBOL: Signifies or represents some truth, idea or fact, but is not itself the thing it represents.

SYMBOL OF GLORY: The Blazing Star in the old lectures. The star in the center represented Deity, hence, the "Symbol of Glory."

SYMBOLISM: Something representing something else, especially truth of a higher order. Derived from the Greek *symbolon*, which was a token of identity verified by comparing with its other half. Symbolism in Freemasonry relates to the philosophical understanding derived from perceiving the proper relationship between the material and spiritual worlds

T

TEMPERANCE: Moderation in action, thought, or feeling; self-restraint; a habitual moderation in the indulgence of the appetites or passions.

TENETS OF FREEMASONRY: Dogmas; principles, beliefs, doctrines; teachings of Brotherly Love, Relief and Truth. A Tenet is something obviously true; that which is universally accepted without question.

TERRESTRIAL: Belonging to the earth.

TESSELLATED PAVEMENT: Checkered floor of black and white, symbolic of the triumphs and the despairs throughout life.

TETRAGRAMMATON: A Greek word signifying "four letters.' It is a name given by the Talmudists when referring to God or Jehovah.

TOKEN, MASONIC: A sign used for recognition to prove that a man is a Mason.

"TO THAT UNDISCOVERED COUNTRY FROM WHOSE BOURNE NO TRAVELER RETURNS": Comes from Shakespeare's Hamlet (Act III, Scene 1).

TONGUE OF GOOD REPORT: Having a good reputation; those who know you report that you are of credit to yourself and to society.

TRACING BOARD: Or emblematic chart. Emblems used to illustrate the lectures.

TRADITION: Derives from the Latin *traditus*, past participle of *tradere*, meaning to give or deliver into the hands of another, to entrust. This word also has Indo-European roots coming from *trans*, meaning to give. With this understanding, tradition is transmission. It is the handing down of knowledge.

TRADITIONAL: According to a belief handed down from generation to generation, but not supported by any sure or exact evidence. A tradition need have nothing of the miraculous in it.

TRANSITION: The passing over from one stage to another.

TRAVELING FROM WEST TO EAST: In Operative Masonry workmen traveled from one job to another and the word "traveling" came to signify a form of work. Hence, a Mason works his way toward the East (place of light) by improving himself as he progresses through life.

THREE STEPS: Emblematical of youth, manhood, and age.

TRESTLE BOARD: The carpet or board upon which the Master inscribes the designs for guidance of the Craft. In the present day it refers to the meeting notice sent to the membership.

TRIALS, MASONIC: Are held in Masonic courts of law in which testimony is heard and the accused either found innocent or guilty. In some jurisdictions, it is the allegation that are found to be "True" or "Not True".

TROWEL: The Working Tool of the Master Mason. Symbolically, to spread the cement of Brotherly Love to fit the capstone to complete the building.

TUBAL CAIN: Artificer in brass and iron. The first Master Craftsman, son of Lamech and Zillah. See Genesis IV:22.

TUSCAN: One of the Five Orders of Architecture, originated in Tuscany, an area of southern Italy

TYRE: City of Sidonian Empire which is only 120 miles by sea from Jerusalem. King Hiram or Tyre provided materials for the building of the Temple.

U

UN-MASONIC CONDUCT: Conduct of a Mason which violates the laws of the Craft and his obligation thereto.

UNDISCOVERED COUNTRY FROM WHOSE BOURNE NO TRAVELER RETURNS: That which lies beyond death; the afterlife. From Shakespeare, Hamlet: Act III, Scene 1.

USUAL VOCATION: Your job; the manner in which you make your living.

V

VISITING: To visit a lodge outside of your "regular" lodge. Visitation Is a privilege and not a right.

V.S.L: Volume of the Sacred Law.

VOUCHING: A brother cannot vouch for the Masonic standing of a brother unless he has sat with him in a Masonic Lodge. Knowledge of his standing or membership in a body requiring Masonic membership as a prerequisite is not grounds for avouchment.

VOUCHSAFE: To grant or furnish; to give by way of reply.

VOID: Empty.

W

WARDENS COLUMNS: At the beginning of the opening ceremonies both columns are down, The Senior Warden's column is elevated down when the WM declares the Lodge open. It is lowered when the Master declares the Lodge called from labor to refreshment, or when, ill the closing ceremonies. The Junior Warden's column is elevated up, when the Lodge is at refreshment. It raised at the moment when the Master declares the Lodge at refreshment, and is lowered when he calls the Lodge to labor. The Senior Warden's column is lowered and raised at the same times.

WAGES, A MASTER'S: Symbolizing the fruits of a man's labors in Masonic work.

WINDING STAIRS: Is one which tries a man's soul. He must approach it with faith believing that there is a top, that by a long and arduous climb he will reach a Middle Chamber. A place of light,

WORKING TOOL OF A PAST MASTER: The plumb line.

WORSHIPFUL: Title of honor and respect.

WORTHY AND WELL QUALIFIED: That by his character and moral living, the candidate is worthy to be a member.

X

Y

YEAR, MASONIC: While the civil calendar reckons from the Year of our Lord and is designated A.D., the Masonic calendar dates from the year when God said, "Let there be Light," and is designated A. L.

YOD: The tenth letter of the Hebrew alphabet.

YORK RITE: The degrees of the lodge, chapter, council, and commandery.

Z

ZEAL: Intensity of purpose and of earnestness.

ZEND-AVESTA: The Persian Volume of the Sacred Law.

ZENITH: The point in heavens directly over head of the spectator; great height.

ZION: The mountain or hill in Palestine on which Jerusalem was built.

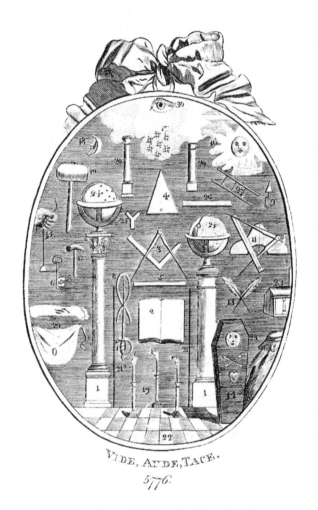

VIDE, AVDE, TACE.

5776.

Published according to Act of Parliament Aug.t 30 1776 by C. Nicoll

Comments may be sent to:
RMSH13@outlook.com

Website:
https://rmsanchez33.wordpress.com/

Facebook:
www.facebook.com/truemasonicexperience

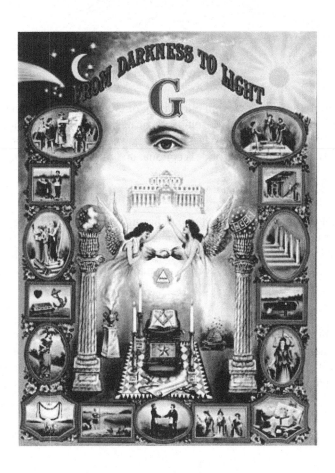

ACKNOWLEDGEMENTS

For brethren interested in purchasing or creating their own lodge jewels, lapel pins or Masonic certificates, I recommend a most reputable firm: The Masters Craft, owned by Brother John Bridegroom. His work exceptional and of great quality and beauty.
Website: www.themasterscraft.net

For brethren interested in purchasing or creating their own aprons or ties, I recommend an amazing and reputable firm: The Craftsman's Apron, owned by Brother Patrick Cradock. His work is of exceptional quality and beauty.
Website: www.craftsmanapron.com

For those interested in more information about the Masonic Restauration Foundation, you can visit their web page. There is a vast amount on information including resources and documents that may be an asset to your lodge, officers, or Masons alike.
Website: http://www.masonicrestorationfoundation.org

Unless otherwise cited, the images in this book are in the public domain. They can be found in the online resource archives of the Grand Lodge of British Columbia and the Yukon.
Website: www.freemasonry.bcy.ca

I had the great honor of having my portrait drawn by the very talented Brother Travis Simpkins, World Renowned artist. I encourage all of you to visit his web page and look at his work.
Website: www.artcrimeillustrated.com

This book would not have been possible without the help of so many people, and I have so many people to thank for this endeavor. My wife Suzette Elizabeth Wunsche Sanchez who is my rock. My entire family who has supported and encouraged me my entire life (los quiero hasta el cielo tin tin). All the brothers that have guided me through this process and have shown me the true meaning of brotherhood, my closest friends, and all of the brethren of St Alban's Lodge No. 1455 & Gray Lodge No. 329. My friends and brothers who have been my travel companions in "Masonic Trips" to all over the world, Clint D. Stevens, Christopher J. Gamblin, and Salomon Lahana. I would also like to thank my publisher, editors, and masons who mentored me through my Masonic Experience such as; Michael D. Nanny, Lawrence E. Tucker, Kenneth B. Fischer, John C. Elkinton, H. Bart Henderson, Richard Sharp, William H. Koon II, Robert Davis, Buddy Baccus, David Lindez, Carl W. Wunsche Sr. Aaron Shoemaker, Christopher Hodapp, Andrew Hammer, Steve Burkle, S. Brent Morris and Arturo de Hoyos. Last but certainly not least, to Rex R. Hutches, and Pierre G. "Pete" Normand, my masonic experience would not have been the same without the two of you. I truly appreciate the years of friendship and guidance. Words cannot describe my gratitude. From the bottom of my heart, THANK YOU ALL.

221

222

NOTES

NOTES

Made in the USA
Monee, IL
20 December 2023